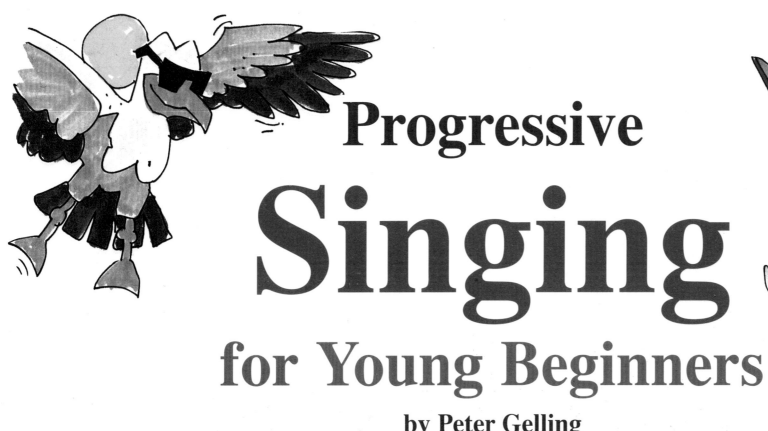

Progressive
Singing
for Young Beginners

by Peter Gelling

Illustrated by James and Hazel Stewart

Published by
KOALA MUSIC ™
PUBLICATIONS

PROGRESSIVE SINGING METHOD FOR YOUNG BEGINNERS
I.S.B.N. 978 1 86469 141 2
Order Code: CP-69141
For more information on this series contact;
LTP Publishing Pty Ltd
email: info@learntoplaymusic.com
or visit our website;
www.learntoplaymusic.com

Let's Practice Together

We have recorded all the songs in this book onto a CD. When your teacher's not there, instead of practicing by yourself, you can sing along with us. Practicing will be much more fun, you can hear all the correct pitches and rhythms, and you will learn faster. Each song is played twice.

- The first time contains the song with the accompaniment and your part (the melody).
- The second time contains just the accompaniment. You can sing your part along with the accompaniment.
- Before each exercise you will hear a note played on a keyboard. This is the note you will begin singing.
- A drumbeat introduction is used to begin each exercise.

Contents

Introduction

Progressive Singing For Young Beginners has been designed to introduce the younger student to the basics of singing and reading music. To maximize the student's enjoyment and interest, the book incorporates a repertoire of well known children's songs along with the use of Sol-fa syllables to help the student identify pitches within the key. All of the songs have been carefully graded into an easy to follow, lesson by lesson format which assumes no prior knowledge of music by the student. Since singing is often accompanied by guitar, piano or keyboard, this book may be used in conjunction with other Progressive Young Beginner books for these instruments, as many of the songs included here are common to these other books.

At the beginning of the book, the student is introduced to the basic principles of posture, breathing and breath control before tackling singing and music reading. Along the way the student learns note and rest values and the $\frac{4}{4}$ and $\frac{3}{4}$ time signatures. The exercises and songs incorporate quarter, whole and half notes and their equivalent rests, as well as eighth notes. The student is taught how to read rhythms, and introduced to basic terms such as bar lines, repeat signs and lead-in notes. New pieces of information are highlighted by color boxes, and color illustrations are used throughout to stimulate and maintain the student's interest.

A Word About Pitch and Timing

Many young students have difficulty in singing pitches accurately. This will improve with practice and experience. It is important to understand the concept of different pitches, but not to worry if the student is unable to accurately reproduce them at first. Relating pitches to the keyboard and learning the Sol-fa syllables will improve the accuracy of pitching, although some students may still take a couple of years to learn to pitch accurately.

One of the most important things about learning music is developing a good sense of time. To get you on the right track from the very beginning, it is strongly recommended that you use a **metronome** to play along with **every time you practice**. There are various types of metronome available, from the old wind-up style metronome to the electronic metronome. Electronic metronomes are recommended because they are more accurate and often have a volume control as well as an earphone input so nobody else hears it except the person using it.

Lesson 1
How We Sing

Everyone has the ability to sing. Some people naturally have better voices than others, but anyone can become a good singer simply by learning to hear and identify sounds and then practicing them. The sound which we know as singing is made by air from an exhaled breath (breathing out) passing over the **vocal cords**, and causing them to vibrate. The vocal cords are small muscular folds of skin located inside the larynx (commonly known as the "voice box"). The sound is then amplified (made louder) and modified by the **resonance spaces** in the mouth and throat and behind the nose. The sound may also be altered by the shape of the mouth, the lips and movements of the tongue as the sound leaves the mouth. Because everybody's anatomy is slightly different, each voice will have its own individual sound both when speaking and singing. The following diagram shows all of the parts of the body which are involved in creating the first sound of a singing note. A singing breath usually starts with the **diaphragm** muscle and then travels upward from there.

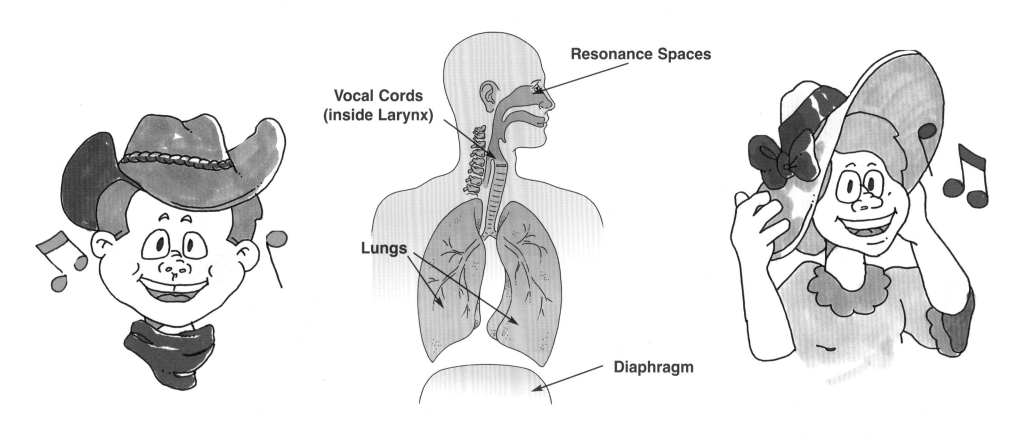

Posture

Posture means the way the body is held (e.g. straight, slumped, etc) and its position when you are sitting or standing. For singing, it is best to **stand** rather than sit, as this allows the most open passage of air for both breathing and singing. Of course, if you are accompanying yourself on piano or keyboard you will have to sit. In this situation, it is essential to sit up straight but relaxed for the best sound. The best posture for singing is demonstrated in the diagram below on the right. Compare this to the incorrect posture position shown on the left.

Incorrect   Correct

In this position, the spine is not straight and the head and pelvis both tilt forward. In this position, it is not possible to move freely or produce the best sound.

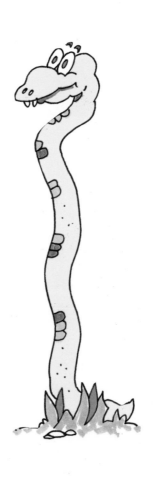

In this position the spine is comfortably straight and in line with the head, legs and pelvis. This position keeps the airways open and makes movement easy and comfortable. Notice that the head is facing straight ahead in a natural speaking position.

Breathing

One of the most important elements of singing is a consistent and relaxed approach to breathing. A good singer always produces a **strong**, **even tone** and sounds relaxed regardless of how high or low the notes are. Shown below is a method of breathing which will help you gain more control over the way you breathe when you are singing.

Step 1

Lie on your back on the floor with your legs straight out. Place the palm of one hand over your navel. Pretend you are blowing your nose. Feel your muscles tighten underneath your hand as you do this. Continue blowing until the muscles are tight. Hold them for a few seconds until you need a breath. As you let go those muscles notice that your hand moves up and you get bigger round the waist as a new breath fills your lungs. Just relax your abdominal muscles and you will breathe in automatically.

Step 2

Stand up and repeat the exercise. Concentrate on the muscles tightening as you breathe out and the feeling of relaxation as you breathe in. Repeat the exercise a few times until you are sure of the feelings as you

Step 3

Breathe out, then in, and then sing a long slow note (the pitch doesn't matter). let the note come out slowly and steadily from your diaphragm, like squeezing a tube of toothpaste from the bottom. Stop, relax, and then repeat the note a few times. Do these exercises for a few minutes each day, and soon you will find you never run out of breath when you are singing.

Remember :

Breathe in = Relax

Breathe out = Gentle effort

Breath Control

When you sing, it is important to control how much of your breath comes out as you sing, so that you don't run out of breath too quickly. This is called **breath control**. Here are some exercises to help you improve your breath control.

Exercise 1

Slowly blow up a balloon, using slow sustained breaths controlled from the diaphragm. The idea is to take a comfortable deep breath and then breathe into the balloon using an even, sustained amount of air pressure.
Repeat this until the balloon is full.

Exercise 2

Sing the sound "**la**" and keep it sounding for as long as possible before you run out of breath. The less force you use as you sing, and the more you breathe from your abdomen, the longer you will be able to keep the sound going.

Melody

When you sing the notes of a song, what you are singing is called a **melody**. Melody is made up of two elements – **pitch** and **rhythm**. Pitch means how high or low the sound is, e.g. most men's voices sound lower and most women's voices sound higher. A bass sounds low and a recorder sounds high. Melodies are made up of notes of various pitches. Rhythm means how long the notes sound for and the timing pattern they create when they are put together. Try singing the melody of any song you already know, even if it is very short. As you sing, listen to the sounds you are making and notice that some notes are higher and some are lower. Also notice any repeating rhythm patterns in the timing of the melody. You can work out the rhythm of a melody by clapping it.

1   High and Low Sounds

Listen to this example on the CD to hear the difference between higher and lower sounds played by musical instruments. The first sound is high and the second one is low. After that, listen to the sounds and say out loud whether each new note is higher or lower than the one before.

Aiming Your Voice

When you sing it is important to aim your voice straight ahead of you, so that your voice comes out with a clear, open sound. The easiest way to do this is to imagine you are speaking to someone the same height as yourself. It is important to stay relaxed and keep looking and singing straight ahead regardless of whether the notes go higher or lower.

Referring to the Keyboard

When you play a melody on an instrument, each note has a specific fingering, so you can always check the pitch by playing that fingering. However, when you sing a melody, it is not possible to see the exact positions of the parts of your body which change the notes (the vocal cords), because they are inside your larynx. For this reason it is a good idea to refer to a musical instrument any time you are unsure of the pitch of a note. In this book, all new notes are shown on a keyboard. If you have a keyboard you can play each new note and then sing it. If you don't have a keyboard, don't worry about the pitches too much, just listen to the songs on the CD and sing along with them. Before each song on the CD, the note you will start singing is played first on a keyboard so you can hear which note to sing.

On any keyboard, the black keys always appear in groups of two or three. The **C note** is a **white key**. It is always on the left hand side of a group of two black keys. Find all the **C** notes on your keyboard.

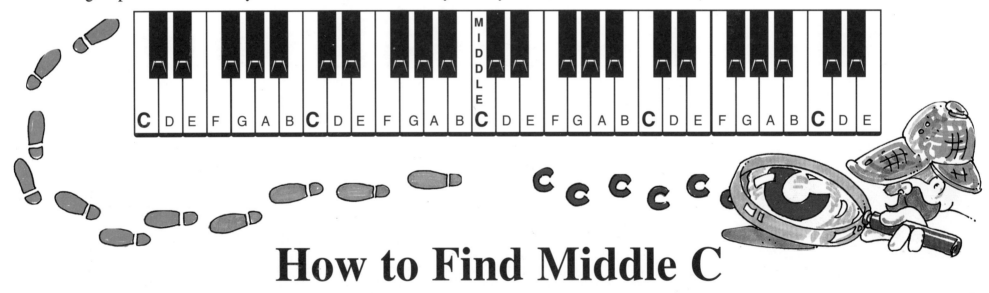

How to Find Middle C

The first note you will learn to sing is called **Middle C**. Middle C is the note in the middle of the keyboard. Since this is a singing book and not a keyboard book, it is not important which finger you use to play middle C (or any other note). The important thing is to listen to the pitch of the note and then copy it with your voice. Many people find this difficult at first, but it gets easier with practice. A good way to become confident of singing the correct pitches is to imagine the sound of each note before you sing it.

Lesson 2
How to Read Music

Music Notes

There are only seven letters used for notes in music. They are: **A B C D E F G**

These Notes are known as the **musical alphabet**.

The Staff

These five lines are called the **staff** or **stave**.

The Treble Clef

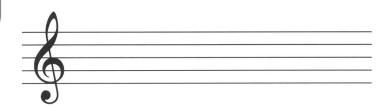

This symbol is called a **treble clef**.
There is a treble clef at the beginning of every line of most vocal music.

CROTCHET

The Quarter Note

This is a musical note called a **quarter note**. It lasts for **one** beat or count.

Count: 1

Music notes are written in the spaces and on the lines of the staff.

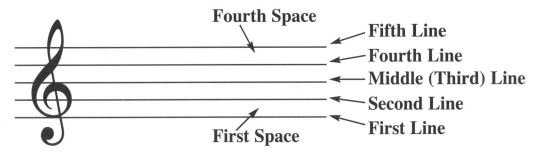

Fourth Space
Fifth Line
Fourth Line
Middle (Third) Line
Second Line
First Line
First Space

The Note Middle C

Middle C is written just below the staff on a short line (called a **leger line**).

Leger Line

Middle C Note

▶ 2   Cat Walk

In this song you will sing eight middle C notes. Clap your hands as you sing each note. **So you know which note to sing, listen to the introduction note to track 2 on the CD**. You could also play middle C on the keyboard if you have one. There are two ways to sing the song; you can sing the name of the note (C, C, C, C, etc) or you can sing the counting numbers (1, 2, 3, 4). It is a good idea to practice both ways.

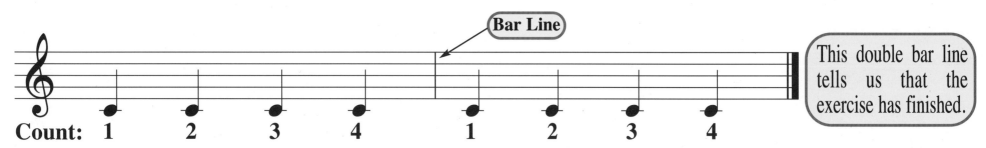

Bar Line

This double bar line tells us that the exercise has finished.

Count: 1   2   3   4   1   2   3   4

Bar Lines

Music is divided into **bars**, or **measures**, by barlines. In the first song there are two bars of music. Each bar contains four quarter notes.

The Four Four Time Signature

These two numbers are called the **four four** time signature.
They are placed after the treble clef.
The $\frac{4}{4}$ time signature tells you there are **four** beats in each bar.
There are **four** quarter notes in a bar of $\frac{4}{4}$ time.

Breathing and Breath Marks

When you are singing, it uses up your breath fairly quickly, which means you will often have to take a new breath between some of the notes. Try breathing every two bars at first. In the song below you will see a sign called a **breath mark**. It looks like this ▼. In the beginning it is a good idea to breathe every time you see a breath mark even if you don't need to. Take a quick, deep breath and then keep singing. Remember to keep a relaxed, upright posture and sing straight ahead of you as if you were speaking to someone the same height as yourself. Tap your foot in time to the music so you don't lose the timing when you breathe.

 3 **Four Four Cats**

This song contains four bars of quarter notes in $\frac{4}{4}$ time. On the recording there are four drumbeats to introduce songs in $\frac{4}{4}$ time. Listen to the introduction note on the CD, hum it to yourself, and then sing with a clear, open voice.

CROTCHET

The Quarter Rest

This symbol is called a **quarter rest**. It means there is **one beat of silence**. Do not sing any note where you see a rest. We place small counting numbers under rests.

Count: 1

BEAT

 4 **Time for a Rest**

A rest is always a good place to take a breath. When you see a rest, hold the note you are singing right up to the beat where the rest occurs, and then take a relaxed breath on that beat. Remember to keep tapping your foot or clapping where you see a rest, even though you are not singing.

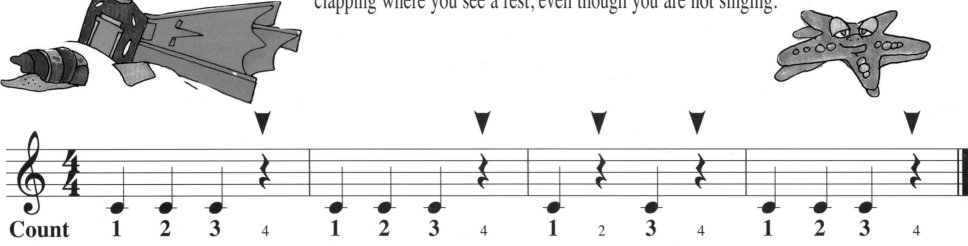

Count   1   2   3   4   1   2   3   4   1   2   3   4   1   2   3   4

Singing Along With the Recording

Most times when you see someone singing in a concert, they have other musicians playing with them. Sometimes they have just a piano or guitar, and other times it may be a whole band or an orchestra. To sing well with other musicians, you need to be able to sing in time with them. A good way to practice singing in time is to sing all the songs in the book along with the recording. Then you can hear how the part you are singing fits in with the other instruments.

The Half Note

MINIM

This is a **half** note. It lasts for **two** beats. There are **two** half notes in one bar of 4/4 time.

Count: **1** 2

The Half Rest

MINIM

Count: 1 2

A black box sitting on a line is called a **half rest**. It means there are **two beats of silence**. Remember that we place **small** counting numbers under rests

▶ **5**   **Halves and Quarters**

MINIM   *CROTCHET*

This song contains half notes and quarter notes. Sing the sound "la" for each note and tap your foot on each beat to help you keep time. If you have trouble with the timing, clap your hands each time you sing a new note.

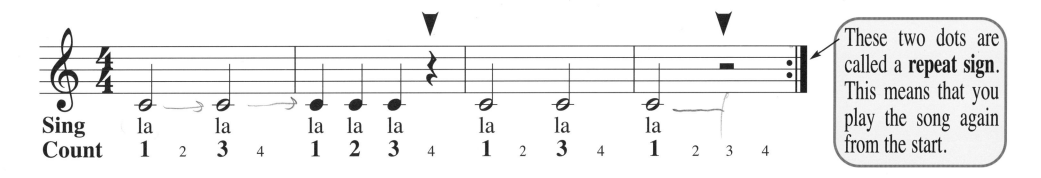

These two dots are called a **repeat sign**. This means that you play the song again from the start.

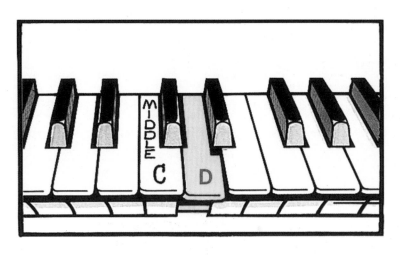

The Note D

The Note **D** is written in the space under the staff.

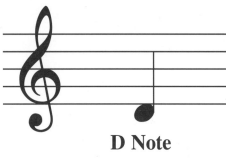

D Note

  6   **Raining Cats and Dogs**

Listen to the this song on the recording to hear the correct pitches and sing along with it. Sing "la" for each note as you go through the song the first time, and then sing the names of the notes (**D** and **C**) as you repeat the song.

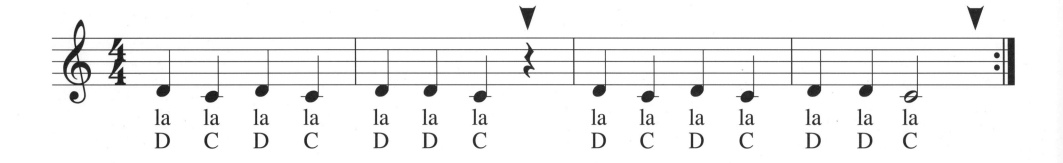

Sol-fa Syllables

So far, you have sung the names of the notes (C and D) and the sound "la" for each song in the book. When you say or sing a single sound like "la" it is called a **syllable**. All words are made up of syllables. For example, the name Mary contains two syllables: Ma-ry. There are particular syllables which can help you learn to sing and hear the difference between different pitches. These are called **sol-fa syllables**. Each syllable matches a different musical pitch. The sounds of these syllables are **do**, **re**, **mi**, **fa**, **so**, **la**, and **ti**. They are a bit like the musical alphabet, because each syllable goes with a different note. The first syllables we will learn are **do** (Pronounced "doe") and **re** (Pronounced "ray"). **Do** is C and **re** is D.

▶ **7**   **Do Re Do**

As you go through this song, sing **do** for every **C** note and **re** for every **D** note. If you are unsure of the sounds of the syllables, listen to the singer on the recording and imitate the sounds you hear.

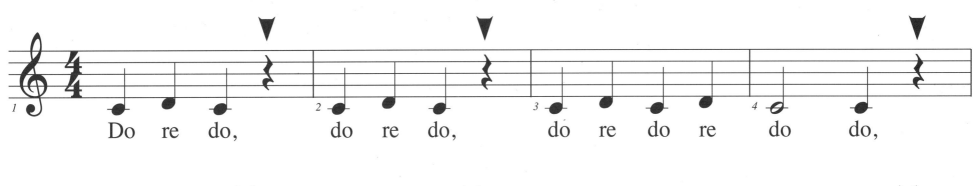

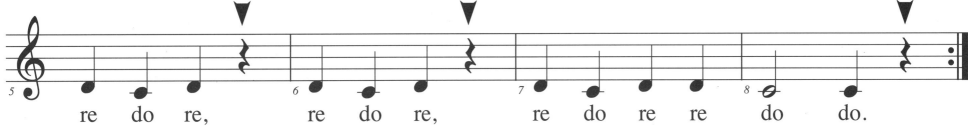

Lesson 3
The Note E (mi)

The Note **E** is written on the first line of the staff

E Note

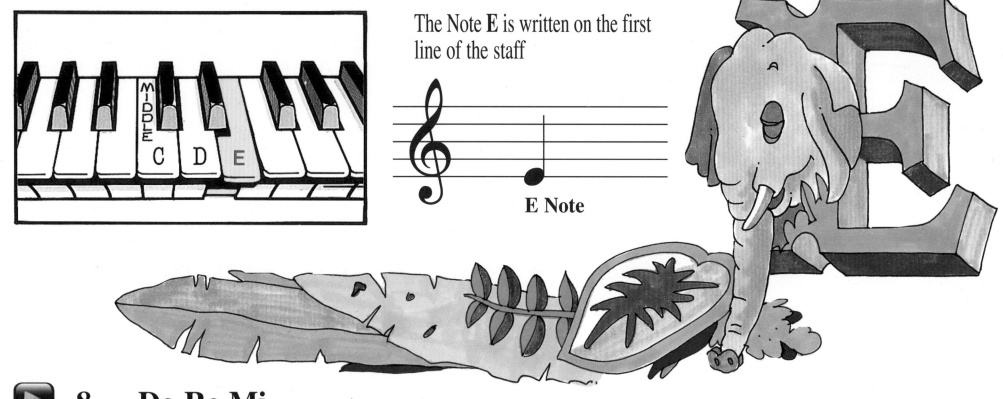

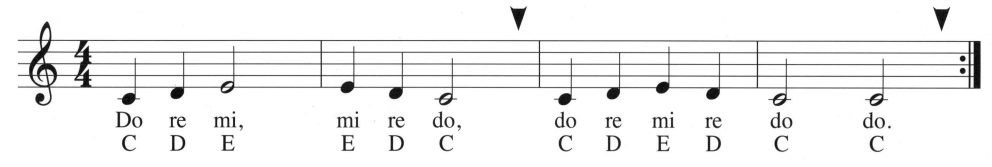

▶ **8   Do Re Mi**

The sol-fa syllable for the note **E** is **mi** (pronounced "me"). Sing this song twice, using the syllables **do**, **re** and **mi** the first time you go through it, and then sing the names of the notes (**C**, **D** and **E**) the second time through.

Diction

Diction means the way you say or sing words. If you are talking to someone and you don't speak clearly, they won't understand what you are saying. It is the same with singing, so it is important to express each word clearly as you sing. As mentioned in lesson 1 you will need to stand up straight and relaxed, and aim your voice straight ahead when you sing, so that your voice comes out with a clear, open sound. The sounds of the words are formed by movements of your mouth, lips and tongue as the air leaves your mouth. Listen carefully as you sing, to make sure you are pronouncing all the words or syllables clearly. When you do this, you are singing with good diction.

9   Merrily

Once again, there are two ways to practice this song. The first time you go through it, sing the words written under the notes (called the **lyrics**) and the second time, sing the sol-fa syllables (**do**, **re**, and **mi**).

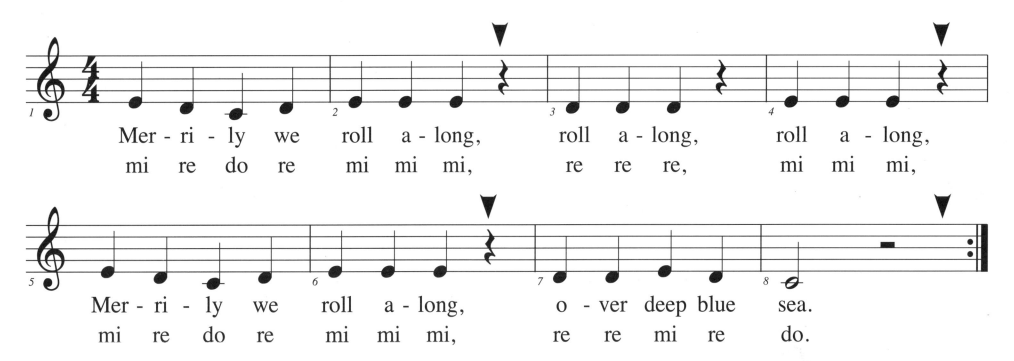

10   Elephant Walk

Remember to sing each new song along with the recording so you can hear how your part fits with the other instruments.

Do   do   re   mi   do   mi   re,   do   do   re   mi   do   do.

The Whole Note

This is a **whole** note. It lasts for **four** beats. There is **one** whole note in one bar of $\frac{4}{4}$ time.

Count: **1**   2   3   4

11   In the Light of the Moon

Do   do   do   re   mi   re,   do   mi   re   re   do

Lesson 4
The Note F (fa)

The Note **F** is written in the first space of the staff.

F Note

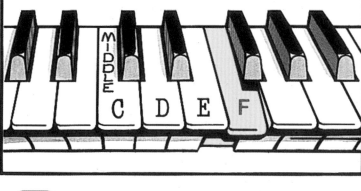

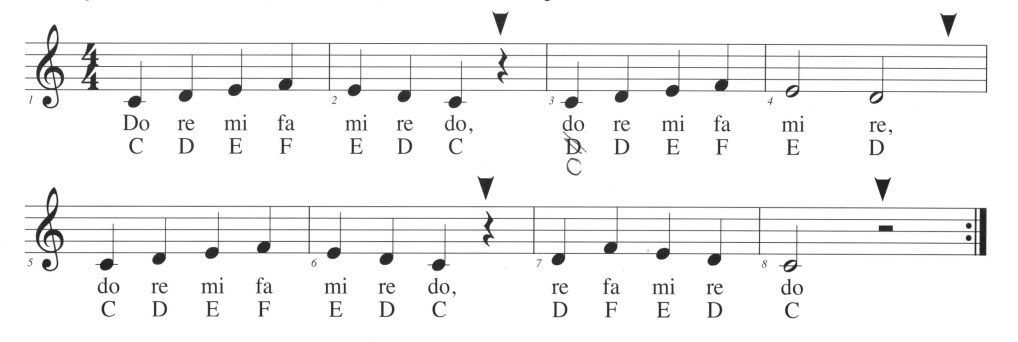

12   Do Re Mi Fa

The sol-fa syllable for the note **F** is **fa**. Sing this song twice, using the syllables **do**, **re**, **mi** and **fa** the first time you go through it, and then sing the names of the notes (**C**, **D**, **E** and **F**) the second time through.

Do re mi fa mi re do, do re mi fa mi re,
C D E F E D C D D E F E D

do re mi fa mi re do, re fa mi re do
C D E F E D C D F E D C

The Note G (so)

The Note **G** is written on the second line of the staff.

G Note

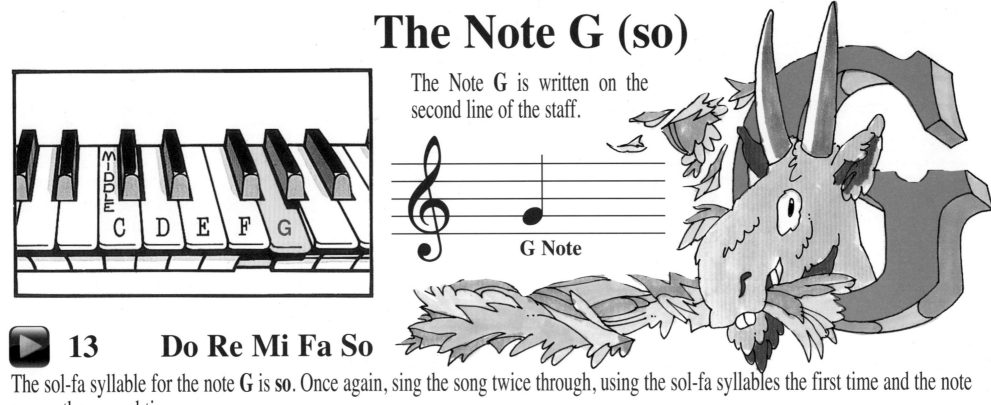

▶ **13**   **Do Re Mi Fa So**

The sol-fa syllable for the note **G** is **so**. Once again, sing the song twice through, using the sol-fa syllables the first time and the note names the second time.

Do re mi fa so — so fa mi re Do
C D E F G — G F E D C

do re mi fa so fa so, — so fa mi re do
C D E F G F G — G F E D C

14   Mary Had a Little Lamb

This song is similar to "Merrily", which you learnt in lesson 3. The difference is the **G** note (**so**) in the fourth bar. There is also an extra note in the sixth bar, which means you will either have to take a very quick breath after the word "lamb" or else wait till the end of the song to take a new breath.

Ma - ry had a lit - tle lamb, lit - tle lamb, lit - tle lamb,

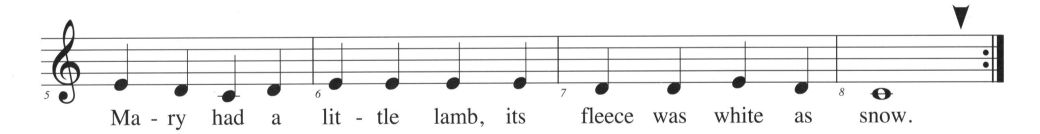

Ma - ry had a lit - tle lamb, its fleece was white as snow.

The Common Time Signature

 This symbol is called **common time**. It means exactly the same as $\frac{4}{4}$.

 ## 15   My House

Here is another song which uses the notes C, D, E, F and G (do, re, mi, fa, so). It is a good idea to practice the song using sol-fa syllables as well as the lyrics. The sol-fa syllables are not written below the lyrics here, so you will need to remember that C is **do**, D is **re**, E is **mi**, F is **fa**, and G is **so**. Be sure you pronounce all the lyrics clearly as you sing.

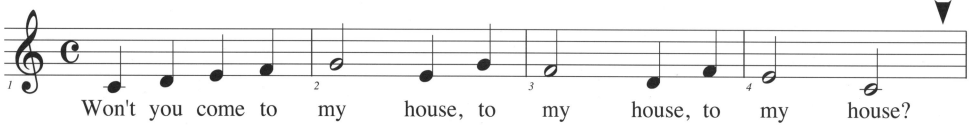

Won't you come to   my   house, to   my   house, to   my   house?

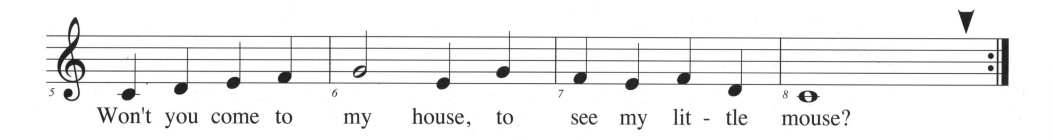

Won't you come to   my   house, to   see   my   lit - tle   mouse?

Lesson 5

The Three Four Time Signature

This is called the **three four** time signature.
It tells you there are **three** beats in each bar.
Three four time is also known as waltz time.

 16 Waltz Time

Before you sing this song, listen to the recording and clap along with the notes, counting 1 2 3, 1 2 3 as you go. Then sing the sol-fa syllables for the song and tap your foot on each beat of the bar as you sing. On the recording there are six drumbeats to introduce songs in ¾ time (two bars).

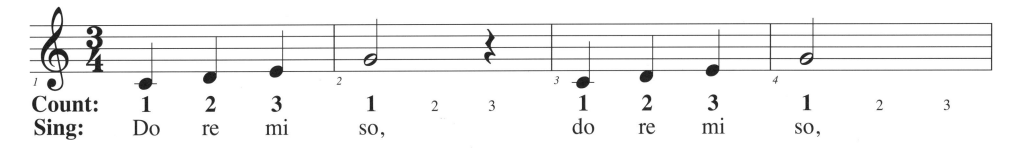

Count: 1 2 3 1 2 3 1 2 3 1 2 3
Sing: Do re mi so, do re mi so,

1 2 3 1 2 3 1 2 3 1 2 3
do re mi so fa mi fa mi re do.

The Dotted Half Note

A dot after a half note means that you hold the note for **three** beats.

Count: **1** 2 3

17 Girls and Boys Come Out to Play

This song contains a dotted half note in the final bar.

18 Little Bo Peep

Don't forget to practice singing each new song along with the recording, and also to practice each song with sol-fa syllables as well as the lyrics.

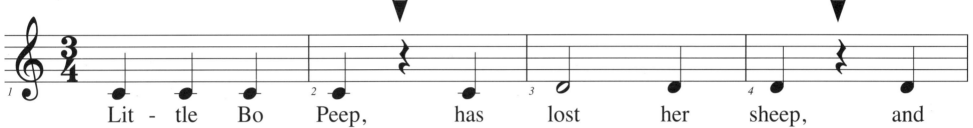

Lit - tle Bo Peep, has lost her sheep, and

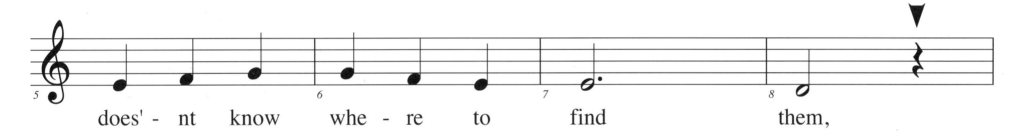

does' - nt know whe - re to find them,

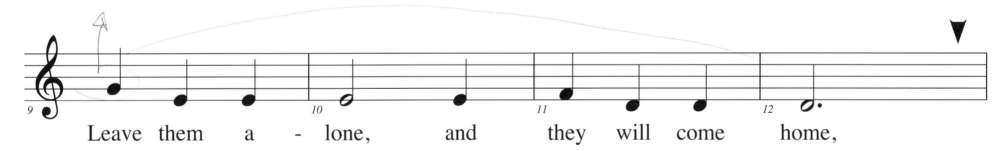

Leave them a - lone, and they will come home,

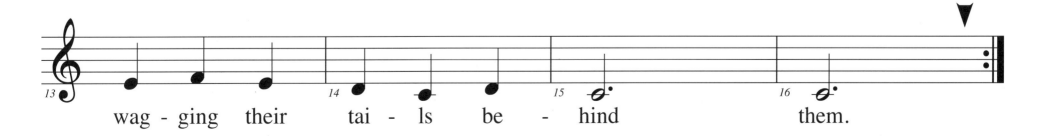

wag - ging their tai - ls be - hind them.

Lesson 6
The Lead-in

Sometimes a song does not begin on the first beat of a bar. Any notes which come before the first full bar are called **lead-in notes** (or **pickup notes**). When we use lead-in notes, the last bar is also incomplete. The notes in the lead-in and the notes in the last bar must add up to one full bar.

 19   When the Saints go Marchin' in.

There are three lead-in notes at the beginning of this song. On the recording there are **five** drumbeats to introduce this song. There are no breath marks written here, so you will have to decide the best places to breathe. Anywhere a rest occurs is usually good. Another good place is at the end of any long note such as a whole note, or at the end of a phrase in the lyrics (where a comma occurs in the lyrics).

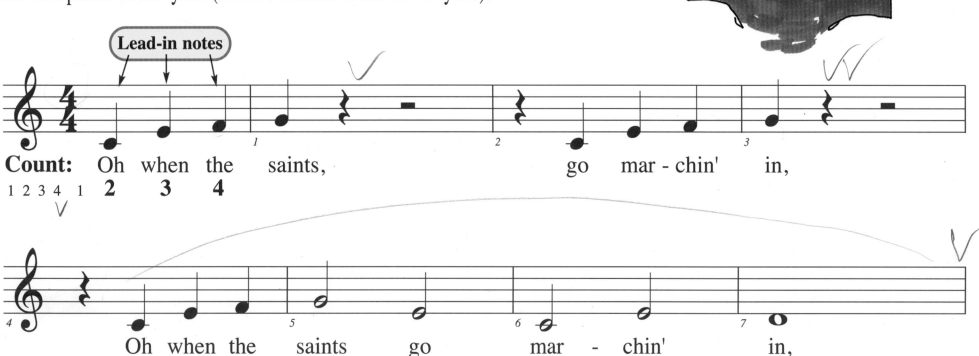

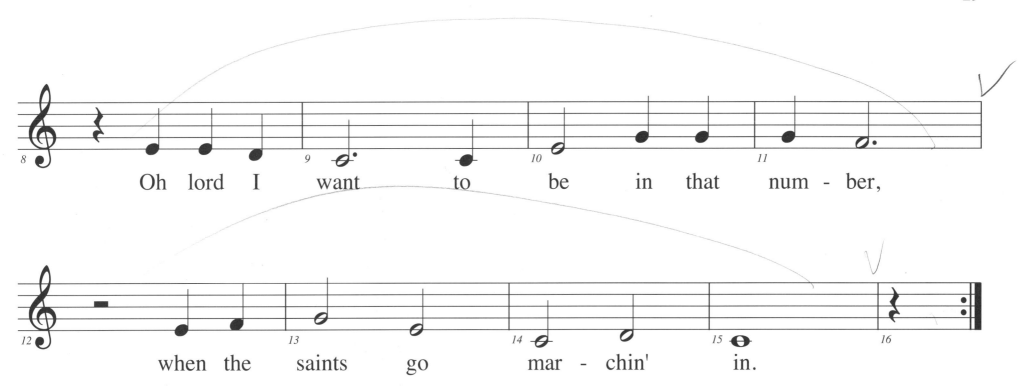

Staccato

A **dot** placed above or below a note tells you to sing it **staccato**. Staccato means to sing a note short and separate from other notes. To sing a note short, stop your breath as soon as the note sounds.

 20   The Cuckoo

Watch the notes carefully as you sing this song, as some notes are staccato and others are not. There is one lead-in note at the beginning of the song. Because of this, there are **five** drumbeats on the recording to introduce this song.

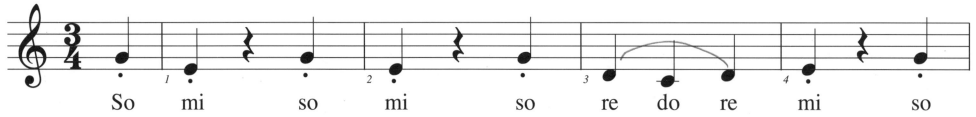

So   mi   so   mi   so   re do re   mi   so

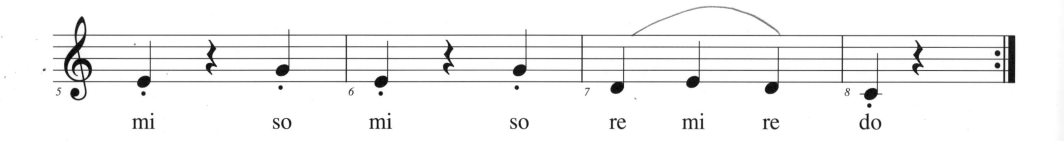

mi   so   mi   so   re   mi   re   do

Lesson 7
The Note A (la)

The Note **A** is written in the second space of the staff.

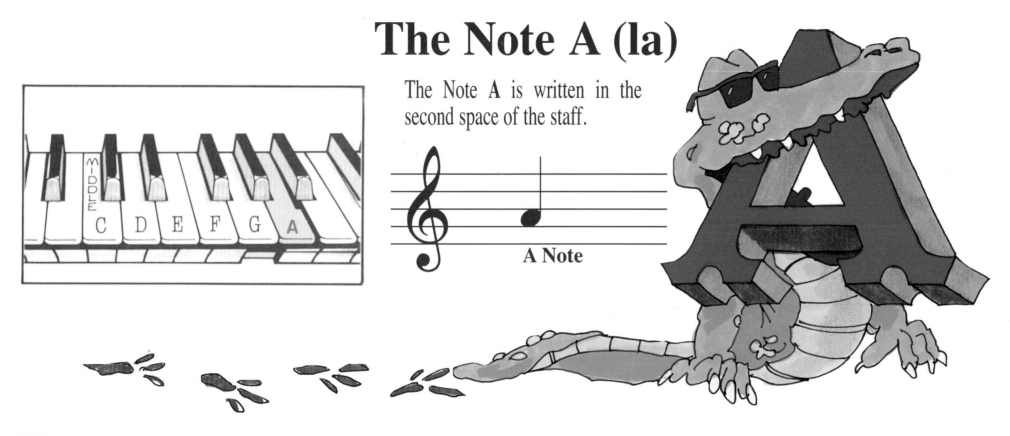

A Note

 21 Do Re Mi Fa So La So

The sol-fa syllable for the note **A** is **la**. As with all new notes, sing the song twice through, using the sol-fa syllables the first time and the note names the second time.

Do re mi fa so la so,   so la so fa mi re do
C   D   E   F   G   A   G   G   A   G   F   E   D   C

22 Twinkle Twinkle Little Star

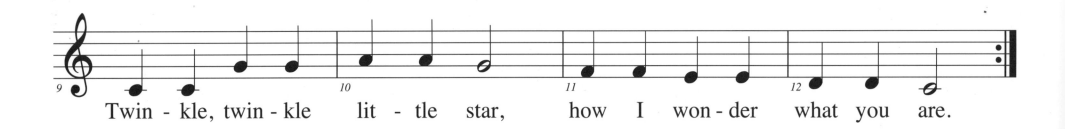

D.C. al Fine (pronounced "fee-nay")

In the last bar of the following song, the instruction ***D.C. al Fine*** is written. This means that you sing the song again from the beginning until you reach the word ***Fine*** (bar 16).

23 For He's a Jolly Good Fellow

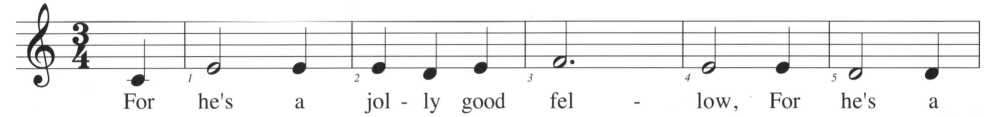

For he's a jol - ly good fel - low, For he's a

jol - ly good fel - low, For he's a jol - ly good fe -

Fine

low, Which no - bo - dy can de - ny. Which no - bo - dy

can de - ny, which no - bo - dy can de - ny.

Lesson 8
The Eighth Note

Tail

This is an **eighth** note. It lasts for **half** a count. There are **eight** eighth notes in one bar of $\frac{4}{4}$ time.

When eighth notes are joined together, the tails are replaced by one **beam**.

Beam

Two eighth notes joined together.

Beam

four eighth notes joined together.

▶ 24 How to Count Eighth Notes

Count:	1	and	2	and	3	and	4	and
Written:	1	+	2	+	3	+	4	+

▶ 25 Snip, Snip

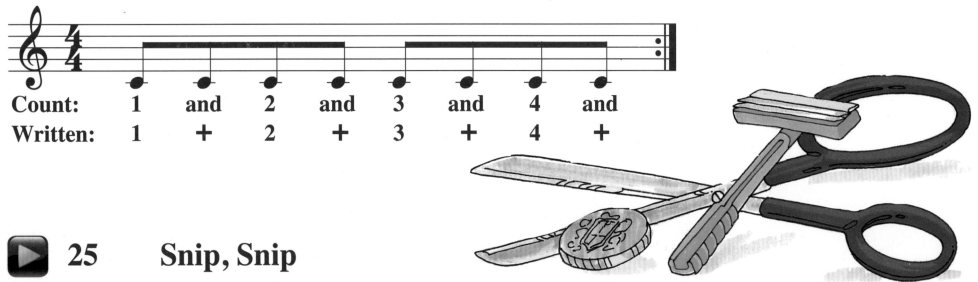

Tap your foot on each beat (the number count) but not on the eighth notes in between the beats.

Cut - ting, Cut - ting, Cut - ting, Snip,   Cut - ting, Cut - ting Cut - ting, Oops!

1   +   2   +   3   +   4   1   +   2   +   3   +   4

Here are two songs which contain eighth notes. Listen to the recording and clap and count the rhythms along with it.

26   Hot Cross Buns

Hot cross buns, hot cross buns, one a pen - ny two a pen - ny, hot cross buns.

Count: 1 2 3 4 1 2 3 4 1 + 2 + 3 + 4 + 1 2 3 4

27   This Old Man

This old man, he played one, he played nik nak on my drum, with a

nik nak pad - dy whack, give a dog a bone, this old man came rol - ling home.

Lesson 9
The Dotted Quarter Note

A dot written after a quarter note means that the note lasts for **one and a half** counts.

A dotted quarter note is often followed by an eighth note.

28

Count   1   2 **+**   3   4

29   **A Dog Called Dot**

Count: My friend has   a   dog called Dot,   She   has   lots   and   lots   of   spots.

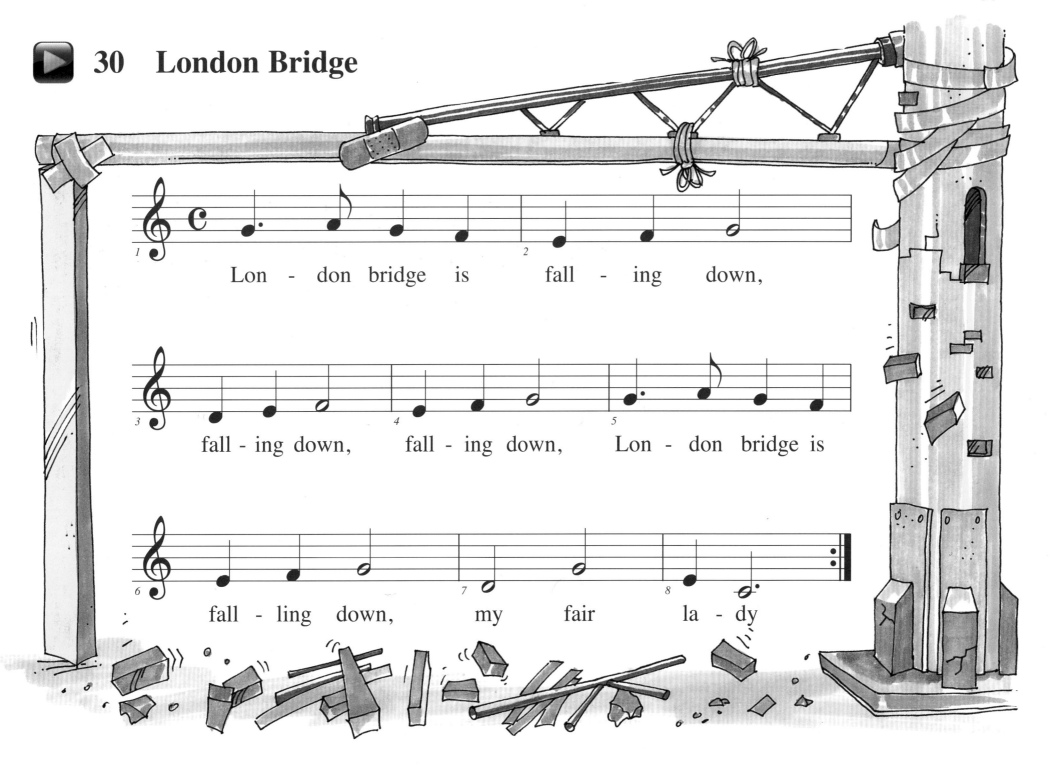

30 London Bridge

First and Second Endings

The next tune contains **first and second endings**. The **first** time you go through the song, sing the **first ending** (⌐1.⌐), then go back to the beginning. The **second** time you go through the song, sing the **second ending** (⌐2.⌐) instead of the first.

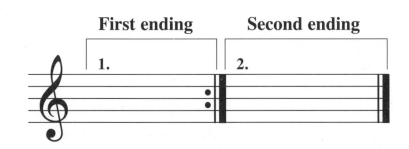

 31   Jingle Bells

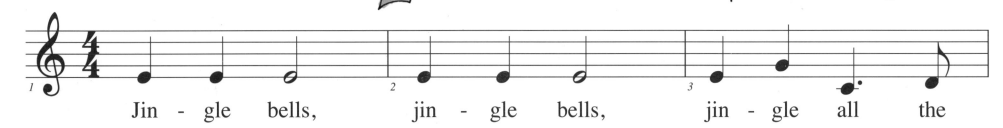

Jin - gle   bells,   jin - gle   bells,   jin - gle   all   the

way,   Oh   what   fun   it   is   to   ride   in   a

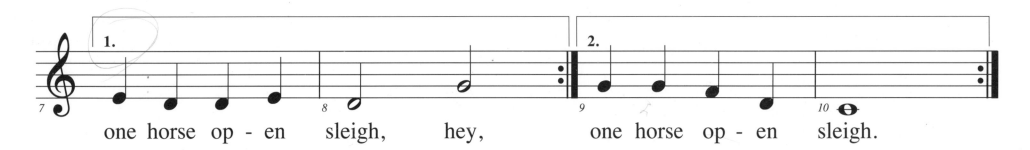

one horse op - en   sleigh,   hey,   one   horse   op - en   sleigh.

Lesson 10
The Note B (ti)

The Note **B** is written on the third line of the staff.

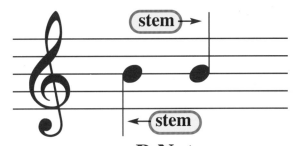

B Note

Notes written below the middle line of the staff usually have their stems going **up**. The stem for the note **B** can go **up or down**.

32   Tea for a Bee

The sol-fa syllable for the note **B** is **ti**.

Do re mi fa so,   la ti so,   la ti so la ti   so fa mi re do.

The Note C
Above middle C (do)

This **C** Note is written in the fourth space of the staff.

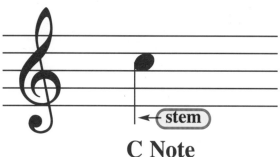

← stem

C Note

Notes written **above** the middle line of the staff usually have their stems going **down**.

The C Major Scale

A **major scale** is a group of eight notes that gives the familiar sound **do re mi fa so la ti do**. You now know all the notes of the **C major scale**.

▶ 33

One Octave

| do | re | mi | fa | so | la | ti | do | do | ti | la | so | fa | mi | re | do |
| C | D | E | F | G | A | B | C | C | B | A | G | F | E | D | C |

The Octave

An **octave** is the range of eight notes of a major scale. The **first** note and the **last** note of a major scale always have the same name. In the C major scale, the distance from **Middle C** to the **C** note above it (or below it) is one octave (eight notes).

34 **Lavender's Blue**

This song uses all the notes of the C major scale. Practice singing it using sol-fa syllables as well as the lyrics.

La - ven - der's blue dil - ly dil - ly, lav - en - der's green,

When I am King dil - ly dil - ly, you will be Queen,

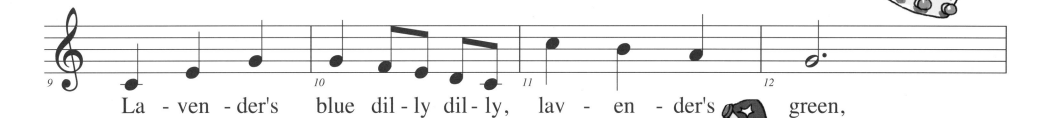

La - ven - der's blue dil - ly dil - ly, lav - en - der's green,

When I am King dil - ly dil - ly you will be Queen.

35   Old MacDonald Had a Farm

Once you know the melody to this song, try singing some verses with the names of other animals and the noises they make. For a second verse you could sing about **Ducks**, and go "**quack, quack**". For another verse you could sing about **Cows** and go "**moo, moo**", and for another verse you could sing about **Pigs** and go "**oink, oink**".

You can keep the song going as long as you can think of new animals and the noises they make.

Old Mac - Don - ald had a farm, E - I - E - I - O, and

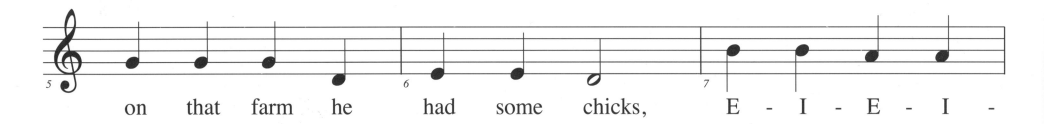

on that farm he had some chicks, E - I - E - I -

O, with a chick chick here and a chick chick there,

here a chick, there a chick, ev'-ry where a chick chick, Old Mac - Don - ald

had a farm, E - I - E - I - O.

Learning More About Music

Music is made up of three basic elements - **rhythm**, **melody** and **harmony**. You have already learned the basics of rhythm and melody in this book. **Harmony** means other notes which accompany the melody. A good example of harmony would be a guitar or keyboard playing chords. Even if you mainly plan to sing, it is a good idea to learn a bit about chords and how they work, so you can understand what other musicians are talking about when they want to accompany you and you can also understand the sounds the instruments are making and why the musicians choose those sounds. The best way to learn more about music is to learn how to play an instrument such as guitar, piano or electronic keyboard. As well as learning chords, this will help you to hear and understand melodies better and give you the tools you need to write your own songs.

The Keyboard

The best instrument for learning about both melody and harmony is the piano or any type of keyboard. This is because the notes appear as black and white keys and this makes it easy to understand what is happening on the keyboard as you play. There are only seven letter names used in music - **A B C D E F** and **G**. These notes are called the **musical alphabet**. On the keyboard, these notes are the names of the white keys. After you reach G, the pattern goes back to A again. If you go higher or lower, you get higher and lower repeats of these notes. An example of this is shown below on the treble staff and then shown on the keyboard below the staff. If you have a friend who plays the keyboard, ask them to show you a bit about what they are doing.

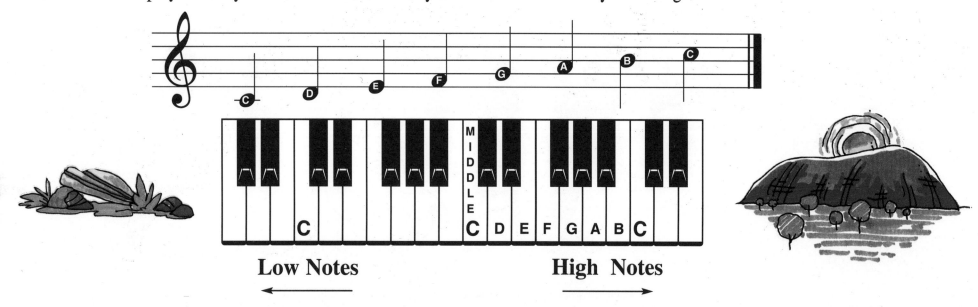

Low Notes

High Notes

'DEARLY BELOVED
WE ARE GATHERED
HERE TODAY
TO GET THROUGH
THIS THING
CALLED LIFE...'

CONTENTS

Mirrorcollection

HEAD OF SYNDICATION & LICENSING: FERGUS McKENNA
MIRRORPIX: mirrorpix.com 020 7293 3700

PRODUCED BY TRINITY MIRROR MEDIA, PO BOX 48, LIVERPOOL, L69 3EB
ISBN 9781910335505

MANAGING DIRECTOR: STEVE HANRAHAN
COMMERCIAL DIRECTOR: WILL BEEDLES
EXECUTIVE EDITOR: PAUL DOVE
EXECUTIVE ART EDITOR: RICK COOKE
MARKETING AND COMMUNICATIONS MANAGER: CLAIRE BROWN
PRODUCTION: ROY GILFOYLE, SIMON MONK, JAMES CLEARY, MICHAEL McGUINNESS
DESIGN: GLEN HIND, COLIN SUMPTER, COLIN HARRISON,CHRIS COLLINS,
ALISON BARKLEY, BEN RENSHAW
WRITERS: CHRIS BRERETON, CHRIS McLOUGHLIN
PRINTED BY: ACORN PRESS

THE ENIGMATIC PRINCE

Loved by millions, yet never really known outside his trusted circle. Intensely private, yet a flamboyant showman. The artist who will forever be known as Prince was a creative genius whose music transformed the world

Imagine taking the finest songwriter, the most enigmatic performer, the best guitarist and the hardest-working producer and combining them in one person.

Fortunately for us, we do not have to imagine. That person was Prince.

When it was announced on Thursday, April 21, 2016, that the American icon had passed away at his Paisley Park home, the musical world was again plunged into mourning.

The death of David Bowie earlier this year was difficult enough to comprehend and now this. Another musical icon taken, way before his time.

Prince was - and remains - one of the biggest musical stars to ever grace the planet.

He suffered from childhood epilepsy and suffered from terrible seizures. However, over time the seizures stopped and he made it his life's work to "be as noisy and flashy as I could" to make up for lost time.

He did not let us down.

Prince Rogers Nelson exploded onto the music scene in the 1980s; an enigmatic figure who had seemingly been given a gift from the musical gods.

There was nothing he could not do, nothing he could not play or sing, no dance move he could not pull off.

And audiences across the world could not get enough.

Modern day musical superstars reach out to their fans through social media, filling Twitter and

Instagram with snippets of their lives aplenty. Yet, throughout his career, Prince stood alone and away from the noise that came with worldwide fame.

Can anyone claim to have really known him, ever really worked him out?

That was all part of his monumental appeal. He gave little away, preferring to allow his music to do the talking.

And what music he produced.

In many ways, he offered us the soundtrack to the 1980s and beyond.

In an era of arena-gods, when the likes of Madonna and the aforementioned Bowie played to tens of thousands, Prince somehow managed to join them in playing huge crowds, but with an intimacy and privacy that gave the impression he was playing a tiny club back in his home town of Minneapolis, Minnesota.

Musical icons are well-known for their tendency to exaggerate their own success, or importance, but when Prince declared, "I am a musician. And I am music" he was forgiven. Because he was right. His music oozed danger and sex appeal, it could not be pinned down to one genre.

Was he a funk performer or a soul singer? Was he a rock star or a pop pin-up?

Was he a lyricist first and singer second – or the other way around?

Nobody knew then and nobody knows now, such was his versatility, creativity and wonderfully perceptive ear.

Some people are simply born to entertain and Prince was definitely one of them. He knew it too, spending his teenage years honing his skills before attracting the interest of companies such as Warner Brothers and Columbia Records.

Prince signed with Warner and managed to immediately have complete control over his output. This was almost unheard of in the dictatorial days when record companies kept their performers on a tight leash. On his debut 1978 album, For You, Prince was credited on the sleeve with having played 27 different instruments across the tracks on the album.

27. *That* is the scale of genius we are discussing here.

His 1979 eponymously-named album went platinum, thanks to the success of tracks such as Why You Wanna Treat Me So Bad and I Wanna Be Your Lover.

The intense, personal album was full of passion and spoke of wider human truths of love, sex and heartbreak.

It was a sign of things to come.

As the 1980s progressed, Prince's music continued to stun – and thrill – the public.

He was the James Dean of the musical world. Every song, every dance move, every performance seemed to overflow with sex appeal, with a dark energy, with a desire to leave his audiences wowed and – let's be honest – turned on.

Prince, like Bowie, seemed to understand that less is very, very much more when it comes to developing and honing a public persona.

Because he stayed quiet, and refused virtually all interview requests, his fans had to fill the vacuum left by his silence themselves.

As a result, he meant a million different things to a million different people.

The only element of interaction Prince wanted was via his many albums and subsequent tours.

1999 was released in 1982 and went multi-platinum, containing hits such as Little Red Corvette and 1999 as well as the lengthy Automatic and Let's Pretend We're Married.

Both of those tracks are well over seven minutes long, proving Prince's willingness to ignore musical convention and follow his own path.

It was a formula that worked – and worked most successfully – on his next album, Purple Rain, released in 1984 with his backing group, The Revolution.

Alongside Michael Jackson's Thriller, Purple Rain is *the* album of the 1980s and contained hit after hit after hit.

The first release, When Doves Cry, set the tone for the success of the album before the likes of Let's Go Crazy, Purple Rain and Take Me With U cemented both Prince and Purple Rain in the very highest superstar category, selling over 20 million copies worldwide.

ABOVE Prince, pictured at the Brit Awards in February 1985, when he was at the height of his commercial peak

"WAS HE A FUNK PERFORMER OR A SOUL SINGER? A ROCK STAR OR A POP PIN-UP? NOBODY KNEW, SUCH WAS HIS CREATIVITY

ABOVE Performing at the Skanderborg Festival in Denmark, August 2013

LEFT Prince played a total of 98 dates on his Purple Rain North America tour in 1984/85

In trademark guitar solo pose during the Purple Rain tour in Detroit, Michigan, 1985

 Prince careered through the rest of the 1980s on a high, swept along by acclaim from fans and critics alike as he continued to evolve and change his musical style to suit his whim, mixing jazz and pop, R'n'B and rock.

The Revolution were disbanded and replaced by the New Power Generation in 1991 but the 1990s were a decade marked by huge creative rows with Warner Brothers about his musical direction, control and style.

When Prince appeared with the word SLAVE written on his face at the Brits in 1995, it meant the battle that had been brewing for some time with his record company paymasters had gone public.

Determined to wrest ownership of his songs from the label, Prince had begun to deliver albums quicker than Warners wished to release them.

They then refused to market The Gold Experience in 1994 – his latest, greatest release since Sign o' The Times seven years earlier. Enraged, Prince effectively buried his past, renaming himself as an unpronounceable symbol, meaning he was widely referred to as The Artist Formerly Known As Prince, TAFKAP for short, and refusing to play Prince material live.

The shows continued to woo delighted fans and

> # THE 1990s WERE A DECADE MARKED BY HUGE CREATIVE ROWS ABOUT HIS MUSICAL DIRECTION AND STYLE

ABOVE In San Francisco, California, one of the dates on The Parade Tour, 1986

receive rave reviews as he treated audiences to thrilling performances packed with new material.

Finally free after reaching a legal settlement with Warners, he fulfilled a longtime ambition by releasing a triple CD Emancipation in 1996, celebrating his marriage to Mayte Garcia as he ended his period of 'slavery'.

With the increased domestic availability of the internet, Prince was an early adopter and his huge Crystal Ball retrospective became the first album to be distributed on the web.

Prince then set up the New Power Generation Music Club, ensuring the immediate release for his music as he put out a range of material including jazz albums and instrumental collections.

With the ending of his Warners publishing contract in 2000, he once again assumed the Prince moniker.

The pioneering groundwork reaped rewards with his Musicology tour and album in 2004 as he became the highest earning musician of the year.

Prince's artistic renaissance continued apace with the superb 3121 album, 21 nights at London's O2 Arena and the jaw-dropping 2007 Superbowl performance viewed by 140 million.

Although Prince's reluctance to share his life with the wider world may have given the impression he was not as prodigious as he once was, last year, fans were treated to three new albums via his website and now we have the seamless blend of rock and soul that is 20Ten.

20Ten is Prince perfection and has been widely hailed as one of his finest albums. Unfortunately, the music has now stopped playing.

Following the 57-year-old's passing, the world seemed to come to a standstill and some fans even speculated that Prince had even foreseen his own death.

Prince, who was found unresponsive in a lift in Paisley Park mansion, bizarrely referenced an 'elevator' in his hit song Let's Go Crazy, as well as telling a crowd on the Saturday before his death to

"THE WORLD SEEMED TO COME TO A STANDSTILL AND SOME FANS EVEN SPECULATED THAT PRINCE HAD FORESEEN HIS OWN DEATH

"wait a few days" before praying for him.

Exactly what he meant by that we will never know, just as the autobiography Prince was penning will now forever remain tragically unfinished.

That book might have given us a glimpse inside the mind of this remarkable, unknowable man, this versatile workaholic, this creative inspiration, this visionary, this virtuoso.

And while we will have to wait for eternity for Prince's memoirs, he did at leave us his music.

And for that alone, we thank him endlessly.

BELOW Prince performing on stage at Wembley, July 1988

EARLY DAYS OF LITTLE PRINCE

For a man with two musicians as parents and who was named after a band, Prince was always set for a future behind a microphone.

The star's father, John Nelson, played piano in a jazz band called the Prince Rogers Trio so when his son arrived on June 7, 1958, it seemed appropriate to name him Prince Rogers Nelson.

"I named my son Prince because I wanted him to do everything I wanted to do," John once said.

John was married to Mattie Della Shaw, an Italian-American singer but the couple split when Prince was two and he was brought up by John.

"My mom's the wild side of me," Prince once said.

"She's like that all the time. My dad is real serene. It takes the music to get him going. My father and me, we're one and the same."

Prince suffered childhood epilepsy and later told how, before the seizures stopped, he tried to "compensate" by being "as noisy and flashy as I could".

His parents' divorce had a profound influence on him too. Prince was first given a guitar by his father and he immediately escaped into a world of chords and melodies where he taught himself the basics.

His reaction to his parents splitting up was to continue to develop as he mastered one instrument after another, eventually being able to play over 20 different types of instrument.

As Prince grew up in Minnesota, he was bullied and developed anger issues.

He said: "I was very bitter when I was young. I was insecure and I'd attack anybody. I couldn't keep a girlfriend for two weeks."

However, as well as being a notable musician, he was also an outstanding basketball player.

He attended Minneapolis' Bryant Junior

High and Central High in the '70s and played American Football, baseball, particularly excelling at basketball.

His former basketball coach Richard Robinson said: "Prince was an excellent player; he was like the sixth or seventh man. He was an excellent ball handler, a good shooter and very short."

Prince's musical talent was clear for all to see and he joined a band called Grand Central.

Over time, Prince developed into Grand Central's lead singer and frontman, eventually changing the band's name to Champagne, and he was starting to realise how much he enjoyed the attention - and adoration - of an audience.

As his teenage years progressed, it became clear to Prince that he could make a

career out of music if he got his big break.

By 1976, he was creating demo tapes and sending them out far and wide until they caught the attention of a Minneapolis businessman by the name of Owen Husney, who immediately recognised his potential.

He signed him up and eventually helped him gain a meeting with Warners Brothers, where the duo negotiated Prince's first contract deal the year after.

Prince was ready to change the world and Husney remembers a remarkable musical talent.

"He was that sort of Beethoven kind of talent," Husney said.

"This is not going to go away, this is not 'oh, we're so sorry, he died and that was great; there's going to be an everlasting future".

27 THINGS

YOU MIGHT NOT HAVE KNOWN ABOUT PRINCE...

13
He wrote his first song, Funk Machine, aged seven – a whole half a century ago.

15
Prince played guitar on Madonna's Like A Prayer – but you wouldn't know, because he wasn't credited.

02
He had a space set aside which he called The Knowledge Room – a library of religious books.

14 He thought playing guitar gave him his full head of hair, telling the Daily Mirror: "I'm convinced all that electricity racing through my body made me keep my hair."

01
Prince was just 5'2" tall.

16 In 1995 he changed his name to the unpronounceable symbol ♀ (also known and copyrighted as Love Symbol #2) as a way of striking back against his label, Warner Bros, who he blamed for low sales.

17 Staff at Paisley Park reportedly called him 'the dude' during this time.

03 Prince was a huge fan of the show New Girl, starring Zooey Deschanel, and once wrote to her to tell her he only watched two things on TV – New Girl and the news. Following this, he made a special guest appearance on the show in February 2014.

18 He was a devout Jehovah's Witness, baptised in 2001 – and he even went door-to-door. In 2003 a woman in Minnesota opened her door to discover the legend standing in front of her home.

04 In 1984 he became the second artist to have a number 1 album, movie and song in the USA at the same time – after the Beatles.

19 When he performed on Saturday Night Live, he swore during a song – and nobody noticed. It became the only show where 'the F bomb' was dropped twice.

20 He recorded an entire album's worth of songs after meeting actress Kim Basinger and falling head over heels, even cancelling a tour to work on it so he could impress her.

05 Prince wrote the song Nothing Compares 2 U, which was made famous by Sinead O'Connor. It was about the sister of his bandmate, Wendy.

21 In 1989 Prince's half-sister sued him, claiming that the lyrics to U Got The Look were written by her. The judge finally sided with the music star after a long court battle.

22 In 2010 he said: "The internet's completely over." He refused to stream songs on Spotify and sell them on iTunes.

23 He told Rolling Stone magazine in 1985 that he was once so poor, he would stand outside McDonalds and smell food because he couldn't afford to eat it.

06
During his early years with the Revolution, his favourite meal was said to be spaghetti and orange juice.

07 There is an urban legend that he had ribs removed so he could perform oral sex on himself.

24 He also wrote Manic Monday for the Bangles.

25 Prince was just blocks away from John Lennon's murder in December 1980.

08 He's had many names – Skipper, as a boy – then Jamie Starr, Christopher Alexander Nevermind, The Purple One. Joey, ♀ and The Artist Formerly Known as Prince /TAFKAP.

26 He developed an alter ego, who was known as Camille. The vocals on the track If I Was Your Girlfriend from Sign O' The Times are said to be that of Camille.

09 After he wrote the song Kiss, he gave it away – but soon took it back after he heard the backing track the other band had added to the song.

10 Prince is actually his real name. He was born Prince Rogers Nelson on June 7, 1958.

11 Prince had a Willy Wonka moment – in 2006, Universal hid 14 purple tickets inside his album. Fans who found it were invited to attend a private performance at his home.

12 He admitted he had a 'wild side' and that his mum, Mattie Shaw, was responsible for it.

27 He lost a child, a boy, in November 1996. The baby died at just one week old from a rare genetic condition, Pfeiffer Syndrome.

START OF A REVOLUTION

Bursting on to the scene in the early 1980s, the world had seen nothing quite like Prince Nelson Rogers. Charismatic and enigmatic, his unique sense of style and soul soon proved an irresistible combination. He came from Minnesota, but before too long, he'd have the whole world eating out of his hands...

Prince performing on stage at the Joe Louis Arena in Chicago in November 1984 as part of his Purple Rain tour

PRINCE
ON HIS MOTHER'S ASPIRATIONS FOR HIM

"She wanted me to go to school, go to college – she sent me to a bunch of different schools. I always had a pretty high academic level, I guess... She always tried to send me to the best schools, but that was pretty much my second interest. I didn't really care about that as much as I did about playing. I think music is what broke her and my father up, and I don't think she wanted that for me... Musicians, depending on how serious they are, they're really moody. Sometimes they need a lotta space, they want everything just right sometimes, y'know. My father was a great deal like that, and my mother didn't give him a lotta space. She wanted a husband per se." (1981)

Strutting his stuff in
Chicago in 1984

Wowing the Wembley crowd
in the summer of 1986

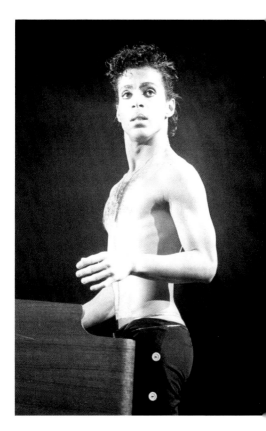

PRINCE
ON RONALD REAGAN

"Thank God we got a better
President now, with bigger balls than
[Jimmy] Carter. I think Reagan's a
lot better. Just for the power he
represents, if nothing else. Because
that also means as far as other
countries are concerned." (1981)

ON WHETHER WHITE
PEOPLE UNDERSTAND
HIS ART

"No, of course they don't. How many
black people understand? White
people are very good at categorising
things – and if you tell them anything
they'll remember it, write books
about it. But understand? You have
to live a life to understand it.
Tourists just pass through." (1983)

ABOVE Looking as suave as ever at the National Indoor Arena in Birmingham

OPPOSITE Striking among the silhouettes in Paris in the summer of 1988

PRINCE
ON BEING MATURE

"Act your age, not your shoe size."

ON SEEKING CONTROL OF HIS MUSIC FROM HIS RECORD COMPANY

"One time in London I walked up to Michael Stipe. I said, 'Do you own your masters?' No, I didn't say hello. He looked scared. He started stuttering. He said, 'I don't know.' I said, 'You need to and you should help me get mine.' He just said, 'Have a nice day.' That was it." (1988)

PRINCE
ON HOW TO BE COOL

"Cool means being able to hang with yourself. All you have to ask yourself is 'Is there anybody I'm afraid of? Is there anybody who if I walked into a room and saw, I'd get nervous?' If not, then you're cool." (1990)

ON LOOKING OUT FOR HIMSELF

"What if everybody around me split? Then I'd be left with only me, and I'd have to fend for me. That's why I have to protect me." (1990)

ABOVE AND LEFT Wowing Wembley Arena again with his backing dancers

LEFT A rapturously received show at Meadowbank in Edinburgh, 1993

PRINCE
ON HIS LOVE OF EXPERIMENTATION

"Making hits is the easiest thing I could do. But it's like taking a ribbon for a race someone else won. I can't do that. I can't repeat myself." (1991)

ON THE SHEER VOLUME OF HIS WORK

"I can't wait four years between records. What am I going to do for four years? I'd just fill up the vault with more songs." (1991)

PRINCE
ON THE BOND WITH HIS BAND

"When Jon Bon Jovi asked me if he could do a song with my band, I went, 'What? No!' It was like he wanted to make love to my woman." (1991)

ON HIS MOVIE GRAFITTI BRIDGE

"It was one of the purest, most spiritual, uplifting things I've ever done. It was non-violent, positive and had no blatant sex scenes. Maybe it will take people 30 years to get it. They trashed The Wizard of Oz at first, too." (1991)

Prince looking smart at the NEC in Birmingham, 1988

PRINCE
ON NEGATIVE ATTITUDES

"I always see myself described as arrogant or pretentious. I just do what I want. I don't consider that arrogance. We should stop arguing and stop attacking each other. The first time I heard sing, I went, 'Hey, you got to quit that – today!' But I had to stop myself. How can I say she shouldn't sing? Maybe she feels a strong need to express herself." (1991)

RIGHT Back in the capital and thrilling the Wembley crowd in 1988

PRINCE
ON COLLABORATING WITH WOMEN

"Women want to work with me more often than men. Women understand me better. They're less threatened by me." (1991)

ON A LACK OF MUSIC EDUCATION

"Nobody's learning how to make music, how to read and write it, and how to play. I worry that we're raising a whole generation that's going to turn out nothing but samples and rehashes." (1991)

LEFT On stage with iconic guitar in Detroit in 1985
ABOVE Wembley 1990

TOP Arms aloft after a triumphant LA show, 1985

ABOVE The Prince juggernaut hits Wembley

LEFT Performing during The Nude Tour at the NEC in Birmingham, June 1990

PRINCE OF PASSION

We've heard about the man himself, but what about the women in Prince's life? Ex-wife Matye Garcia was one of several who shared highs and lows with the star...

Prince's ex-wife Mayte Garcia joined the rest of the world in expressing her shock at the passing of her former husband.

The couple married in 1996 when Mayte was just 22. She had been a backing dancer for Prince and the two fell in love, although tragedy was to overshadow their marriage.

Mayte said: " Prince was my first crush and my first love, but we didn't start to get serious until I turned 18. He was very respectful."

Mayte and Prince welcomed their first child shortly after they married but their son, Boy Gregory, died just a week after birth due to Pfeiffer syndrome, a rare defect of the skull.

That loss, followed by a miscarriage not long afterwards, tore the grieving couple apart.

"To lose two babies is really scary," Mayte said. "It really caught on me emotionally, physically, everything. It took me at least 15 years to get over it and still, to this day, I miss my son.

"I believe a child dying between a couple either makes you stronger or it doesn't. For me, it was very, very hard to move forward and for us as a couple I think it probably broke us."

After she and Prince separated in 2000 she began a two-year relationship with Mötley Crüe rocker Tommy Lee. Three years ago she adopted her daughter, Gia, now four-and-a-half.

Refusing to be known merely as "Prince's ex-wife" she is now a bona fide Hollywood actress.

When not acting, Mayte rescues animals. She has set up two dog sanctuaries and has six dogs, two cats and five birds at her LA home.

Mayte lived with Prince at Paisley Park, his famous 70,000 sq ft mansion in Minneapolis, where he was found dead.

TRAGEDY OF PRINCE'S CHILDREN

As is often the case, no amount of fame, money or success can make superstars immune from tragedy and Prince suffered several major blows during his lifetime.

After losing Boy Gregory, Prince - in complete shock - went on the Oprah Winfrey show with Mayte and the pair pretended he was still alive, giving her a tour of his playroom.

When the chat show host asked about the boy, the Purple Rain singer replied: "We have a long way to go; there will be many more children..."

Mayte later explained how they were simply unable to process the death.

"We had to show people that we were strong, that we had faith, and that we would try again," she said. "But I didn't really want to speak to anybody. I was physically distraught. When you miscarry your body is freaking out, like 'Why can't I feed the baby?' so those were the things I went through. Every day was a struggle even to breathe."

THE WOMEN HE LOVED

Prince's love life has long been a hot topic of discussion and the women who dated him often ended up being his muse.

The 57-year-old star, married twice during his life – to Mayte Garcia from 1996 to 2000 and Manuela Testolini from 2001 to 2006.

Over the years he's been linked to pop stars, supermodels and a whole host other stunning girls.

Here's a look at Prince's lovers over the years..

Denise Matthews

The Purple Rain hitmaker met Denise, also known as Vanity, at the 1980 American Music Awards and he later asked her to be the lead singer of his band Vanity 6.

She released her autobiography, Blame It On Vanity, in 1997 and claimed Prince was the only man she ever truly loved.

Variety broke the news of her death earlier this year, reportedly from kidney failure. She was also 57. Prince paid a touching tribute to his musical protege at one of his gigs after learning of her death.

Manuela Testolini

Prince first met Manuela Testolini in Minneapolis while she was working for the charity Love4OneAnother in 2001. She was 24 and the superstar was 43 when they tied the knot the same year.

She reportedly founded production company Gamillah, which also featured a line of designer candles.

Talking about her marriage to Prince, she said: "It was a very eye-opening experience to see what show business was all about. It was never my desire to be in the spotlight, but it was a great experience because it allowed me to start my own business."

Prince's marriage to the beauty lasted five years and she filed for an amicable divorce in 2006.

Anna Fantastic

Anna Garcia, known as Anna Fantastic, is an English actress, singer and model who was the star's live-in girlfriend in the early 1990s.

She was just 16 when she met the musician at his concert in London and a year later she moved into his home in Minneapolis, Minnesota.

On her 18th birthday, he reportedly gave her a pink cashmere coat, the inspiration for the song 'Pink Cashmere' released in 1993.

Delilah

Prince reportedly started dating British singer-songwriter Delilah in 2014, after visiting London for a string of secret gigs.

The pair had allegedly been friends for two years after he saw a video of her on YouTube and invited her on his tour.

The 24-year-old star was seen at his gig at Ronnie Scott's in London with guests including Rita Ora, Kate Moss and Noel Gallagher.

Delilah attending the British Fashion Awards

Charlene Friend

The Raspberry Beret hitmaker then dated interior designer Charlene Friend, but things got messy when she tried to sue him in 2003.

She was an 18-year-old virgin when they first men in a Hollywood bar. He was 14 years her senior and they embarked on a two-year romance.

In her statement, she said: "Prince informed me he took sexual relations very seriously. He believed he was the Messiah and if you engaged in sex with him, you became one with him.

"He would have me dress in his clothing at his whim. His staff were not allowed to look at me and I was not allowed to look at them."

She took legal action for defamation and emotional distress but Prince won in court, proving he was the victim of a "spiteful lawsuit".

Mayte Garcia
The pair were introduced backstage at one of the singer's shows after he'd seen a video of her bellydancing. They stayed in touch and two years later she joined his band and became an integral part of his life.

They married on Valentine's Day in 1996, in Prince's hometown. Mayte, then 22, wore a necklace of the famous Symbol that Prince had adopted as his name. White doves were released as they exchanged vows.

The four-year love affair between the couple culminated in an extravagant marriage ceremony, an outlandish lifestyle and tragically, the loss of two children.

"SHE WAS JUST A FAN WHO POSTED A COUPLE OF MESSAGES AND THEN SUDDENLY SHE WAS WORKING AT HIS PAISLEY PARK RECORDING STUDIOS... AND THEN SHE WAS HIS WIFE."

EXCLUSIVE: LOVE

ON the quiet suburban streets of Minneapolis, he cuts a remarkable figure. Dressed in a tailor-made suit and trademark stack heels, he steps lightly out of his purring limo and, surrounded by four bodyguards, approaches the modest picket-fenced homes.

And to each astonished resident opening their doors to the peculiar group, multi-millionaire superstar Prince quietly asks: "Would you like to talk about Jesus?"

Welcome to the new world of the man who once outraged a nation with the song Sexy MF and who changed his name to a symbol. Gone are the wild parties, the womanising and the bizarre all-purple lifestyle. Instead, 45-year-old Prince's hedonistic excesses have been replaced with door-to-door preaching and Bible study classes.

Credit for this remarkable transformation, the Daily Mirror can reveal, is down to his mother's dying wishes, new wife Manuela Testolini, who, at 27, is 18 years his junior, and his baptism as a Jehovah's Witness.

It is Manuela - the fan-turned-employee-turned-spouse - who has stood by his side as he embraced his new faith and it is she who has helped him return to the musical spotlight after years of obscurity.

This month sees the release of his critically-acclaimed new album Musicology and he recently made a triumphant return to performing at the Grammy awards.

The bid to recapture his position among the pop elite is music to the ears of Canadian-born Manuela.

Prince - who has romanced a string of women, including Sheena Easton, Susanna Hoffs of The Bangles, Madonna, Kim Basinger, Kristin Scott Thomas and Carmen Electra - has never been a big fan of monogamy.

But now, in middle-age, he seems to have adopted it with Manuela.

But the way he and Mani, as she is known, met and married is a strange combination of fairytale and stalker fantasy.

She grew up in a tiny two-bed apartment in a run-down block on the thundering Don Mills Road in Toronto, Canada.

She was a plain teenager who, as a high school student, was known as an avid Prince fan.

Her passion for the diminutive musician continued at York University in Toronto - where she studied for a degree in art - to the detriment of her social life.

FELLOW student Sorayah Kassim-Lakha remembers her regularly playing her hero's hits, particularly If I Was Your Girlfriend and I Wanna Be Your Lover.

"Mani was always very quiet at college," Sorayah says. "She didn't go in for parties and stuff like that.

"She was only ever interested in her art and in Prince. She was obsessed with him. It's all she ever talked about."

Mani was a frequent visitor to the internet fan club alt.music.prince, a forum devoted to her then hero and now husband.

She admitted to being a "lurker" - someone who watches what others say but seldom joins in conversations.

One of the UK fans who did talk to her online was Antony Golding from Bolton, Lancs.

"It's all a bit surreal," he says. "She was just a fan who posted a couple of messages and then suddenly she was

By NICK WEBSTER

working at his Paisley Park recording studios... and then she was his wife.

Manuela graduated from university in the summer of 1998 and soon after she landed her dream job working with the singer. That year, she received a brief credit on Prince's New Power Soul album.

Twelve months later, she became his assistant. Rumours quickly began to circulate that she was more than just a member of staff before his marriage to first wife Mayte Garcia was annulled in May 2000.

Less than three years earlier, Mayte had given birth to the couple's son Gregory, who tragically only lived a week before dying from the rare bone condition Pfeiffer Syndrome, a genetic skull deformity.

SOON after the annulment, Prince, who was once worth £100million, took Manuela with him to Bible study classes with the Jehovah's Witnesses.

After a hush-hush romance, superstar and fan tied the knot in a Jehovah's Witness wedding in Hawaii on New Year's Eve 2001.

A year later, in a private ceremony at the Kingdom Hall in Chanhassen, Minnesota, Prince and Mani were baptised into their new faith in front of the 167-strong congregation.

A small bathtub-sized pool was hired for the occasion. Wearing knee-length robes with swimsuits underneath, they became full members of the church by being immersed in the pool.

Ronald Scofield - one of the elders of the Chanhassen Congregation, Prince's new place of worship - says it was a special day for all.

"Every time one of our members gets baptised it's exciting. But this was exceptionally exciting because it was someone who has made a lot of changes to their life.

"We have watched Prince since he started studying the Bible and noticed a dramatic change. It's something to be very proud of."

The death of Prince's mother, jazz singer Mattie Shaw, was a turning point for the star, who has sold more than 100 million albums.

Her dying wishes were for him to become a Jehovah's Witness, as she had been for most of her life, and to see him married. He tied the knot with Mani week before h

PRINCE'S PASSIONS

EX-WIFE: Mayte Garcia

LOVER: Sheena Easton

AFFAIR: Madonna

WILD: The old Prince

VES POP LEGEND A NEW PURPLE PATCH

The fan who wed Prince and turned him from a sex god into a doorstep Bible basher

HIS PRINCESS: With second wife Manuela Testolini

PLAIN: Mani at uni

...other passed away and six months ...ter the death of his father, pianist ...d bandleader John L Nelson.

As part of his new life, Prince and ...anuela pay weekly visits to the ...sidents of Minneapolis. At times, ...cofield accompanies the couple ...nd their bodyguards.

HE admits it can take a good ...few minutes before stunned ...homeowners recover from ...e shock of finding a superstar at ...heir door.

Speaking publicly about Prince's ...ew beliefs for the first time, Scofield ...onfirms: "He's so well known that ...when he turns up on people's ...loorsteps, it really surprises them.

"To see him in a Christian lifestyle ...s very pleasant. He's doing very well ...nd spiritually he seems to be ...making a great deal of progress, too.

"We go on Bible studies together ...and work in field service, the door-to-door ministry that Jehovah's Witnesses are known for. When you get past the initial shock of actually meeting Prince, he is very persuasive. He uses the scriptures very well."

After a decade of seclusion, the man christened Prince Rogers Nelson is back to being plain old Prince and playing the hits that made him famous such as Purple Rain, Let's Go Crazy and Little Red Corvette.

And no longer is he synonymous with Paisley Park and Minneapolis.

These days, he and Manuela spend much of their time in Los Angeles or the sprawling £3million grey stone mansion he bought at 61 The Bridle Path in an upmarket area of Toronto. At first, mystery surrounded the purchase of the luxury home by a firm called Gamillah Holdings, until it was discovered that the company's president is one Manuela Testolini.

While the couple are away touring the US, builders are constructing a large gatehouse and a new fence, complete with tennis court and pool.

Though it seems a world away, the estate is just a five-minute drive from Mani's parents' tiny apartment.

Despite the age gap and the star's colourful past, Prince has been welcomed with open arms by the Testolini family.

In January, residents of the village of Calabogie – on the outskirts of Ottawa – couldn't believe their eyes when he and Mani arrived in a gleaming limousine for the modest wedding of her sister Daniela to businessman Michael Dykeman. Onlookers say Prince and his wife happily mingled with the other 80 guests during the reception at the Dickson Manor ski lodge.

The singer admits that along with a new wife, he also has a new set of values. "There's no more envelope to push," he says. "I pushed it off the table. It's on the floor. Let's move forward."

PRINCE also says that TV viewers are now bombarded with dirty music videos.

"Back when I made sexy tunes, the sexiest thing on TV was Dynasty and if you watch it now, it's like the Brady Bunch," he explains.

"My song Darling Nikki was considered porn because I said the word masturbate. That's not me any more."

But with the new tour and album to sell, maybe the wife and new beliefs are just another marketing tool being used by one of the world's ultimate showmen.

Among those with a view about the "new" Prince is Minneapolis gossip columnist CJ, who has followed his career for years, much to the annoyance of the artist himself who wrote a song about her called Billy Jack Bitch.

"A lot of credit is being given to Manuela," she says.

"Both his parents died recently, too. And that's the last barrier to realising that you, too, will die. Maybe that's the reason for the change in personality.

"He was always capable of monogamy but the man got bored quickly. The traumatic death of his baby changed all that. It affected him in a big way.

"People are curious as to why he's changed. The joke here in Minneapolis is that it looks like they finally got the medication right."

nick.webster@mirror.co.uk

A DECADE OF DEVOTION

During the 1990s, Prince was one of the music industry's biggest and most loved stars and fans flocked to his concerts wherever he played. His sex appeal, sense of artistic flair and willingness to push the boundaries made him as important, influential and entertaining as ever. As these superb photos show, whenever he played in Britain, Prince went all-out to give his adoring fans the best night of their lives...

Prince captivated his audience at the BBC's Broadcasting House as part of his 'Act II' tour in September, 1993

PRINCE
ON THE MUSIC OF THE FUTURE

"In the future, I might be interactive. You might be able to access me and tell me what to play." (1994)

ON HIS YOUTHFUL EGO

"I had a massive ego. Massive. But that's not such a bad thing. Because at least you're aspiring to be something, you consider yourself great because you want to be great." (1996)

LEFT AND BELOW: Prince merged outstanding musicianship with a unique fashion sense. It made him irresistable viewing

PRINCE
ON RELIGION

"I do feel like a punk, because no-one believes in God anymore." (1996)

ON NATURE

"If you put a loaf of bread on the table, it turns into medicine and to me that is incredible. The bread will eventually take care of itself. That's nature, that's the Truth." (1996)

ABOVE Prince performing during the 'Act II' tour at the National Indoor Arena in Birmingham, July, 1993

OPPOSITE In Scotland, June, 1993

PRINCE
ON THE ROCK AND ROLL LIFESTYLE

"I know those paths of excess, drugs, sex and alcohol - all those experiences can be funky, they can be very funky, but they're just paths, a diversion, not the answer..." (1996)

ON FREEDOM

"I find freedom sexy. I find freedom so sexy I can't even explain it to you. You wake up every day and feel like you can do anything." (1996)

PRINCE
ON LIFE

"Everyone has their own experience. That's why we are here, to go through our experience, to learn, to go down those paths and eventually you may have gone down so many paths and learned so much that you don't have to come back again." (1996)

ON HIMSELF

"I'm no different to anyone. Yes, I have fame and wealth and talent, but I certainly don't consider myself any better than anyone who has no fame, wealth or talent. People fascinate me. They're amazing! Life fascinates me! And I'm no more fascinated by my own life than by anyone else's." (1996)

LEFT Prince performing on the second night of his 'Act II Tour' at the National Indoor Arena in Birmingham in July, 1993

OPPOSITE At Meadowbank, Edinburgh, the week after his Birmingham gigs

PRINCE
ON HIS PLANS

"Not to sound cosmic, but I've made plans for the next 3,000 years. Before, it was only three days at a time." (1996)

ON WORKING IN PRIVATE

"It's a way of cutting the chaos off, cutting off the outside voices. I heard 'Prince is crazy' so much that it had an effect on me. So one day I said, 'Let me just check out.' Here there is solitude, silence – I like to stay in this controlled environment. People say I'm out of touch, but I'll do twenty-five or thirty more albums – I'm gonna catch up with Sinatra – so you tell me who's out of touch. One thing I ain't gonna run out of is music." (1999)

PRINCE
ON HIS NAME CHANGE

"I had to search deep within my heart and spirit and I wanted to make a change and move to a new plateau in my life and one of the ways in which I did that was to change my name and so to divorce me from the past and all the hang-ups that go with it." (1999)

ON EPILEPSY

"I've never spoken about this before but I was born epileptic and I used to have seizures when I was young and my mother and father didn't know what to do or how to handle it, but they did the best they could with what little they had." (1999)

ABOVE Winning the International Male Solo award at the 1995 Brits

LEFT Prince during his opening concert of his first British tour at Wembley Arena

PRINCE
ON HIS RIVALRY WITH MICHAEL JACKSON

"Chris Rock asks: "There's the story of you turning down Bad?" "Well, you know that Wesley Snipes character? That would have been. Now you run that video in your mind." (1999)

ON RUMOURS OF A VAULT OF UNRELEASED MUSIC

"One day someone will release them. I don't know if I will get to release them. There's just so many and I like writing new stuff and we do new stuff all the time." (1999)

LEFT Prince on stage at his
Ultimate Live Experience
Tour at the NEC in
Birmingham, March 1995

PRINCE
ON THE ART OF PERFORMANCE

"You can't go out there unless
you've got the show completely in
shape. It can look pretty wild
onstage, but everyone knows exactly
where they're supposed to be. That
was a lesson I had to learn from
when I was starting out. When we
first went out behind 1999, The Time,
who were opening for us, beat us up
every night. They would laugh about
it; it was a joke to them. Our show
wasn't together. I had to stop the
tour and get things tightened up.
Now me and the band have a certain
relationship with each other, and
every night we make the audience
part of that."

WITH LOVE FROM ME 2 U

While Prince will always be, and will always deserve to be, regarded as a solo artist of incomparable versatility and musical knowledge, he was also never shy of joining forces with other musicians.

He wrote popular songs such as 'When You Were Mine' for Cyndi Lauper, the insanely catchy 'Manic Monday', for the Bangles, he helped Madonna in the late 80s on her 'Like a Prayer' album, playing guitar on three tracks without credit, and Chaka Khan had one of her biggest ever hits when she included Prince's 'I Feel For You' on her 1984 album of the same name.

"I loved him," Khan wrote on Twitter, after hearing Prince had died. "The world loved him. Now he's at peace with his father. Rest in power, @prince, my brother."

Stevie Nicks, after leaving Fleetwood Mac, was also assisted by Prince's genius when he helped her write her hit 'Stand Back'.

However, Prince's biggest and most successful collaboration saw him give Sinead O'Connor a worldwide hit in 1990 with 'Nothing Compares 2 U'.

He had originally written the song for The Family, a funk band Prince set up in 1985, but O'Connor's video - making the most of almost constant playing on the increasingly popular MTV music channel - catapulted O'Connor to overnight fame.

The shaven-headed Irish singer cried real tears in the music video, touched by the emotion of Prince's words and the fact the lyrics reminded her of her dead mother.

Prince wrote for a lot of other pop stars throughout his career including Cyndi Lauper, The Bangles, Madonna, Chaka Khan, Stevie Nicks and Sinead O'Connor

Purple reign in the Super Bowl rain

From being naughty in the 1990s to finding God in the noughties, the last 16 years of Prince's life saw a shift in musical focus. He also embraced the Jehovah's Witnesses and toned down some of the explicitness of his act, but his impact remained far-reaching, not least through a memorable 12-minute set at half-time of Super Bowl XLI in 2007 when he finished with Purple Rain amidst a Miami downpour. Many regard it as Super Bowl's greatest half-time show

Prince in concert at The Electric Ballroom in Camden, London, February 2014

PRINCE
ON A NEW APPROACH TO LIFE

"There is something that happens when you get emancipated. You approach life differently. You eat differently. You respect yourself more. You respect the gift you have been given." (2014)

PRINCE
ON THE INTERNET

"The internet's completely over. I don't see why I should give my new music to iTunes or anyone else. They won't pay me an advance for it and then they get angry when they can't get it. The internet's like MTV. At one time MTV was hip and suddenly it became outdated. Anyway, all these computers and digital gadgets are no good. They just fill your head with numbers and that can't be good for you." (2010)

Arriving for the UK Premiere of The Bourne Ultimatum, at the Odeon West End in London

PRINCE
ON GROWING AS AN ARTIST

"I don't know how any of us grow if we just tread water. The idea is that we keep growing." (2013)

ABOVE Famous UK rock residencies include Eric Clapton's 24 nights at the Albert Hall and Pink Floyd's 14 nights at Earls Court, but Prince's 21 nights in London, at the O2 Arena in 2007, captured the public's imagination

LEFT looking every inch the rock star at Heathrow Airport ahead of flying to New York on Concorde

MIDDLE Did Prince ever look more dapper?

RIGHT performing at the Brit Awards at Earls Court in 2006

There aren't many who can carry off wearing sunglasses at night. Prince could

ABOVE On stage at Wembley in July 1988 (top) and arriving for The Brit Awards in February 1997

PRINCE
ON WRITING SONGS

"It's like listening to a colour and believing that these colours have soul mates and once you get them all together the painting is complete." (2014)

Prince arrives for the annual Vanity Fair Party at Mortons Restaurant, Los Angeles, in 2007

ABOVE & LEFT Prince's reunion with Wendy and Lisa from The Revolution and Sheila E was something of a surprise at The Brits in 2006. He performed Te Amo Corazon, Fury, Purple Rain and Let's Go Crazy

ABOVE "Everything's changed this summer. It doesn't matter who came before or who comes after. From now on, the O2 is Prince's house."

PRINCE
ON GETTING OLDER

"My hat goes off to anybody who can sit down and put their heads together. I am ready for something like that because I am free and I am happy and I have time. There were a lot of things in the way before. I have nothing but time, and I love getting older." (2014)

INSIDE PAISLEY PARK

When the Daily Mirror's Peter Willis went to interview the music legend at his private mansion in 2010, it was even more unusual than he could have imagined

No experience in my life is ever going to be as bizarre as the day I spent with Prince at his Paisley Park retreat.

I was privileged to be given a rare insight into his secretive world, and his first interview with a British newspaper for a decade because the Daily Mirror was exclusively releasing his album 20TEN as a free CD giveaway to every reader.

The rock legend showed me around his famous studio, treated me to a private performance, invited me to jam on stage in his private concert hall and threw a 'party' just for me in his private nightclub.

Our interview, in July 2010, had been on and off for weeks.

Then I was suddenly phoned one afternoon by his manager in London and told he would see me as long as I could get to his fun factory, near Minneapolis... by the following morning.

The manager then added firmly: "DON'T bring a camera, mobile phone or tape recorder – or it's all off."

After a transatlantic dash, I was met by one of his backing singers, Shelby Johnson, waiting to drive me to Paisley Park – an address that was as synonymous with Prince as Neverland was with Michael Jackson.

I had envisaged a gothic purple palace at the end of a winding lane, but it turned out to be a huge white 70,000 square foot building, resembling an industrial complex, on a busy main road. It looked like the last place you would expect

to find Prince's studios, a concert hall and even his own private nightclub.

Prince's mansion looked VERY different on the inside.

Shelby showed me into the lobby, kitted out in the style of a 1950s American diner and, before I had the chance to sit down, Prince strode in, beaming, with hand outstretched.

I was amazed. Where was the superstar entourage – burly security, manic PRs and personal assistants? There was no-one else around.

"Hi," he said, "I'm so glad you could come." His voice was deeper than I expected, he was certainly small (5ft 2in at most), looked almost half his age and was dressed immaculately, if oddly, in white silk trousers, flouncy green silk shirt, an ivory tunic and white pumps (which, I suspect, were stacked).

"You must come and listen to the album," he said. "I hope you like it. It's great that it will be free to readers of your newspaper. I really believe in finding new ways to distribute my music."

He explained that he decided the album would be released in CD format only in the Mirror in the UK. He no longer trusted the record industry and there would be no downloads anywhere in the world because of his battles against internet abuses.

Unlike most other rock stars, he had banned YouTube and iTunes from using any of his music and had even closed down his own official website.

He said: "The internet's completely over. I don't

see why I should give my new music to iTunes or anyone else. They won't pay me an advance for it and then they get angry when they can't get it.

"The internet's like MTV. At one time MTV was hip and suddenly it became outdated. Anyway, all these computers and digital gadgets are no good.

"They just fill your head with numbers and that can't be good for you."

Then he led me to his recording studio in the complex and invited me to sit in his leather swivel chair at the enormous mixing desk.

Wow! I had finally arrived at the epicentre of Prince's world - the scene of fabled all-night recording sessions in which he apparently played up to 27 instruments.

This is where the genius behind classics such as Purple Rain, When Doves Cry, 1999 and Let's Go Crazy created his great music. The walls were a vibrant reddish purple, flickering candles lined every ledge and the smell of incense filled the air.

Prince jabbed a few buttons and hidden speakers burst into life with my preview. He looked at me for a reaction and I told him it was brilliant, as indeed it was.

"This one's called Compassion," said Prince. But, as I tried to jot down the title he looked aghast, grabbed my wrist and pleaded: "Please, please. It's a surprise, don't spoil it for people."

He told me how these were trying times and to emphasise the point, chivvied me into another room, switched on the TV and showed me an evangelical TV documentary blaming corporate America for a range of woes from Hurricane Katrina to asthmatic children.

He said that one problem was that "people, especially young people, don't have enough God in their lives."

He was a devout Jehovah's Witness and even had an area set aside which he had labelled The Knowledge Room. It featured a library of religious books.

With missionary zeal, Prince talked about his beliefs and how he had been door-to-door to convert non-believers. But when I asked him anything remotely personal, he was extremely brusque.

Questions about his childhood were met with: "I don't talk about the past."

On his relationship with his then girlfriend, Bria Valente, he said: "Self interest is on the back-burner now."

And, on late friend/foe Michael Jackson, he simply replied: "Next question."

Time for another surprise. "Come!" he said, and like an excitable Willy Wonka, he led me down corridors, lined with glinting platinum discs, to a lounge where his three talented backing singers, Shelby Johnson, Olivia Warfield and Elisa Fiorilla, were waiting by an ebony futuristic grand piano. I suspected they had been waiting for us for some time.

Prince indicated I should sit down on a solitary seat in the centre of the room as he started singing a rousing track called Act of God... especially for me.

Surreal wasn't the word. I thanked them profusely, Prince smiled and sent me off for dinner. But, as it was 'only' 10pm he suggested we regrouped back there in an hour 'to party'.

As he had a reputation as the Prince of Darkness for not starting gigs until 2am or leaving clubs until dawn, my expectations ran high. When I returned later, he welcomed me warmly into his private nightclub.

It was lavishly kitted out with velvet circular sofas, a dancefloor and there was a chrome stairway up to a balcony.

On two huge screens, at least 20ft high, there were videos of him performing.

But where were the guests? And where was the bar? I was suddenly reminded that he was a strict teetotal vegan as one of those backing singers wandered in... and offered me a glass of still water.

She was closely followed by the other two

"WOW! I HAD FINALLY ARRIVED AT THE EPICENTRE OF PRINCE'S WORLD – THE SCENE OF FABLED ALL-NIGHT RECORDING SESSIONS...

ABOVE Prince's Paisley
Park retreat looked like
an industrial complex
to outsiders but was
very different inside

singers, carrying trays of sliced melon and raw vegetables, which they placed on a long table beside a large Bible. "Help yourself," said one.

Prince arrived with girlfriend Bria, dressed as if she had come to the Oscars, in a shimmering full-length evening gown.

Twice married and divorced, he had been with the singer, who was almost half his age, for three years at that stage.

He produced her first solo album, Elixer, the previous year and she joined the Jehovah's Witnesses. He introduced her, she looked around at the empty nightclub and said: "Sorry, I think I'm a little overdressed!"

They popped out for a minute and returned, with her proudly holding a food blender filled with a banana smoothie, which they poured into glasses for themselves.

Just when it couldn't get any more bizarre, Prince clambered behind a stack of video equipment under the stairs and started showing

us 1970s clips from the US TV show, Soul Train, of his heroes such as Marvin Gaye and Barry White.

He urged his guests - all five of us - to dance, and the spirited backing singers began moving around the dancefloor as if they were having the time of their lives.

Prince emerged occasionally to study the screens a bit closer. But every time I tried to chat to him he darted back under the stairs, shouting: "Too many questions."

From his agility, it was clear rumours he needed a double hip op after too much dancing on high heels were unfounded. But, after an hour or so, he had had enough of his party and asked me to follow him.

Off we went again, down yet more corridors of platinum discs, we passed iconic guitars and that famous bike from Purple Rain.

He had decided to take me to his private concert hall which, with a capacity of more than 1,000 people, was awesome.

ABOVE Prince's Paisley
Park retreat looked like
an industrial complex
to outsiders but was
very different inside

PRINCE **63**

Pride of place was a huge Love Symbol #2 - the name of the symbol he had changed his name to when he fell out with his old label Warners.

He said: "It's what I always dreamed of when I was a young musician, playing in the basement. Music is my life. It's my trade. If I can't get it out of my head I can't function. Someone told me they saw me at my peak, but how do they know when my peak is? I think I'm improving all the time. When I listen to my old records I'm ashamed of how I played then."

He added earnestly: "Playing electric guitar your whole life does something to you. I'm convinced all that electricity racing through my body made me keep my hair."

Prince thought playing the guitar had kept him youthful.

Then he shouted: "Get yourself an instrument." And next minute, he was arranging an impromptu jamming session... with him at his famous purple grand piano, flanked by his backing singers and me on the drums.

It didn't take long for him to realise I had no rhythm.

Just two minutes into the Beatles classic, Come Together, when I thought I was really getting into my stride, I became aware he was staring over at me in disbelief and wincing.

"Stop! Stop! Stop!" he shouted and slammed his hand down on the piano. Laughing, he added: "Have you ever seen The Apprentice on TV? Cos you're fired!"

I protested. 'Let's take it from the top again,' I suggested. But it was too late. I'd blown it.

Still, there can't be many people who've been hired and fired by Prince, all in the space of two minutes.

As Prince said farewell, having nothing to lose, I cheekily pulled out a camera and asked for a picture.

He shook his head. "It's much better in the memory bank," he said. Then he turned to a backing singer and said. "The picture will make your eyes look red and they will use it really big."

A few days later, on returning to London, I got a clearer idea of why he had managed to fall out with so many people in the entertainment industry.

Prince, who was renowned as a perfectionist, tried to force us to scrap the album - apparently because he had gone off one of the tracks - but the CDs had already been pressed and we had watertight contracts.

Sadly, for all the time I spent with him, I don't think I got much closer than anyone else to understanding the brilliant, crazy, little genius whose music defined an era.

HE WAS STARING OVER AT ME IN DISBELIEF AND WINCING. 'STOP! STOP! STOP' HE SHOUTED. 'YOU'RE FIRED!'

Heading home. Prince
leaving Heathrow
Airport for New York

LIFE IN MOMENTS

From penning his first song at just seven years old to his induction in the Rock and Roll Hall of Fame in 2004, take a look at Prince's extraordinary story, full of life, love, loss and some breathtaking albums from a true musical icon

1991

October 1 – His new band, the New Power Generation, debut on the hit Diamonds and Pearls album, which gives Prince his fifth US No.1 single, *Cream*.

1990

November 20 – Prince's fourth and final film, Graffiti Bridge, proves a critical and box office flop – although the accompanying album proves a bigger hit.

1989

June 20 – His nine-track soundtrack to Batman is released, which yields sales of 4m+ and a US No.1 single, *Batdance*. As part of the deal to complete the soundtrack, his record company force him to sign away the publishing rights to them.

1988

July 8 – The critically-acclaimed 84-show Lovesexy world tour – the album which spawned *Alphapet St* – begins in Paris. It also proves his final extended outing in the US for 16 years. Despite big audiences, the tour loses money due to the use of expensive sets and props – and subsequent transportation costs.

1993

June 7 – Celebrates his 35th birthday by changing his name to a symbol, asking to be known as the Artist formerly known as Prince.

1995

Begins scrawling SLAVE on his face in protest at being tied to his Warner Bros record contract, who be blames for falling sales. Changes his name again to the unpronouncable symbol, also known and copyrighted as the Love Symbol.

1996

February 14 – Marries Mayte Garcia – for whom he had dedicated 1994's *The Most Beautiful Girl In The World*, but suffers tragedy when son Boy Gregory passes away in October at just a week old from the rare genetic condition, Pfeiffer syndrome. They would split in 2000.

2001

Now known again as Prince, he marries Manuela Testolini (who files for divorce five years later), having also become a Jehovah's Witness in the same year, even going door-to-door to spread the word.

1958

June 7 – Born in Minneapolis, Minnesota, USA, Prince Rogers Nelson, the only son of musicians John Lewis and Mattie Della Shaw.

1976

Having written his first song, Funk Machine, aged seven, he performs in bands from his early teens, including 94 East. His demo tape impresses record labels, with Warner Bros agreeing a three-record $1m contract.

1978

April 7 – First album *For You* – on which he sang and played all the instruments, is released, but makes little impression commercially.

1979

January 5 – Performs for the first time with his first band at the Capri Theatre in his home city. October sees the release of his self-titled platinum-selling second album, which spawns million-selling single *I Wanna Be Your Lover*, which peaks at No.11 in the US charts.

1987

March 31 – The iconic *Sign o' the Times* album is released, which Prince tours extensively overseas with a backing band featuring the remnants of The Revolution. On September 11 his self-designed $10m Paisley Park Studios, half an hour outside his home town of Minneapolis in Chanhassen, is officially opened.

1984

June 25 – *Purple Rain* is released, selling 13m in the US alone and spending 24 weeks at No.1. The project yielded an Oscar-winning movie (released a month later) and iconic hit singles including *When Doves Cry*; at one point he has the US No.1 album, single and film at the same time, the first solo artist to achieve the feat.

1982

October 27 – Worldwide breakthrough album *1999* – his fifth LP – is released, the first in which his band, The Revolution, were acknowledged. It includes hit singles *Little Red Corvette* and the title track.

1981

October – In support of fourth album Controversy he opens for the Rolling Stones on their US Tour. The LP was the first on which he began to use abbreviated spelling. He also forms side project band The Time, who would go on to release four albums.

2004

March – Inducted into the Rock and Roll Hall of Fame, in the same year in which his *Musicology* album, released with Columbia Records, went double platinum – his most commerically successul since Diamonds and Pearls – and spawned two Grammy Awards and a successful North American tour.

2007

February 4 – Plays the Super Bowl half-time show, and performs a record-breaking 21 concerts at London's O2 Arena – both receiving rave reviews from critics and fans. The following year he wins his seventh and final Grammy.

2010

July 10 – Releases 33rd studio album 20TEN in the UK, which is made available free by the *Daily Mirror*. Refuses to allow his songs to be streamed on Spotify and be allowed for sale on iTunes. His final album, HITnRUN Phase Two, was released in December 2015.

2016

April 14 – His final performance, at the Fox Theatre in Atlanta. He is found dead in his home a week later.

1958 - 2016

DISCOGRAPHY

Back catalogue of all the Prince releases to hit the UK charts

ALBUMS

DATE FIRST CHARTED	TITLE	ARTIST	LABEL	PEAK POSITION	WEEKS ON CHART	WEEKS @ NO.1
27.10.1982	**1999**	PRINCE	WARNER BROTHERS	30	00	00
21.07.1984	**PURPLE RAIN**	PRINCE AND THE REVOLUTION	WARNER BROTHERS	07	86	00
08.09.1984	**1999**	PRINCE	WARNER BROTHERS	30	22	00
04.05.1985	**AROUND THE WORLD IN A DAY**	PRINCE AND THE REVOLUTION	WARNER BROTHERS	05	20	00
12.04.1986	**PARADE**	PRINCE AND THE REVOLUTION	WARNER BROTHERS	04	26	00
11.04.1987	**SIGN 'O' THE TIMES**	PRINCE	PAISLEY PARK	04	32	00
21.05.1988	**LOVESEXY**	PRINCE	PAISLEY PARK	01	34	01
01.07.1989	**BATMAN (OST)**	PRINCE	WARNER BROTHERS	01	20	01
01.09.1990	**GRAFFITI BRIDGE**	PRINCE	PAISLEY PARK	01	08	01
24.08.1991	**GETT OFF**	PRINCE AND THE NEW POWER GENERATION	PAISLEY PARK	33	03	00
12.10.1991	**DIAMONDS AND PEARLS**	PRINCE AND THE NEW POWER GENERATION	PAISLEY PARK	02	51	00
17.10.1992	**SYMBOL**	PRINCE AND THE NEW POWER GENERATION	PAISLEY PARK	01	21	01
25.09.1993	**THE HITS/THE B-SIDES**	PRINCE	PAISLEY PARK	04	16	00
25.09.1993	**THE HITS 2**	PRINCE	PAISLEY PARK	05	31	00
25.09.1993	**THE HITS 1**	PRINCE	PAISLEY PARK	05	28	00
27.08.1994	**COME**	PRINCE	WARNER BROS	01	09	01
03.12.1994	**THE BLACK ALBUM**	PRINCE	WARNER BROS	36	05	00
18.02.1995	**PURPLE RAIN**	PRINCE	PAISLEY PARK/ WARNER	18	09	00

DATE FIRST CHARTED	TITLE	ARTIST	LABEL	PEAK POSITION	WEEKS ON CHART	WEEKS @ NO.1
18.02.1995	**DIAMONDS AND PEARLS**	PRINCE	PAISLEY PARK/ WARNER	25	07	00
11.03.1995	**BATMAN - OST**	PRINCE	PAISLEY PARK/ WARNER	81	02	00
07.10.1995	**THE GOLD EXPERIENCE**	(SYMBOL)	WARNER BROS	04	01	00
04.09.1999	**THE VAULT... OLD FRIENDS 4 SALE**	PRINCE	WARNER BROS	47	01	00
11.08.2001	**THE VERY BEST OF**	PRINCE	WARNER BROS	02	39	00
01.05.2004	**MUSICOLOGY**	PRINCE	COLUMBIA/NPG	03	07	00
01.04.2006	**3121**	PRINCE	UNIVERSAL	09	04	00
02.09.2006	**ULTIMATE**	PRINCE	WARNER BROS	06	22	00
11.10.2014	**ART OFFICIAL AGE**	PRINCE	NPG/WARNER BROS	08	03	00
11.10.2014	**PLECTRUMELECTRUM**	PRINCE & 3RDEYEGIRL	NPG/WARNER BROS	11	02	00
24.09.2015	**HITNRUN - PHASE ONE**	PRINCE	NPG	50	02	00

SINGLES

DATE FIRST CHARTED	TITLE	ARTIST	LABEL	PEAK POSITION	WEEKS ON CHART	WEEKS @ NO.1
19.01.1980	**I WANNA BE YOUR LOVER**	PRINCE	WARNER BROTHERS	41	03	00
22.01.1983	**1999**	PRINCE	WARNER BROTHERS	25	08	00
09.04.1983	**LITTLE RED CORVETTE**	PRINCE	WARNER BROTHERS	54	11	00
30.06.1984	**WHEN DOVES CRY**	PRINCE	WARNER BROTHERS	04	15	00
22.09.1984	**PURPLE RAIN**	PRINCE AND THE REVOLUTION	WARNER BROTHERS	08	09	00
08.12.1984	**I WOULD DIE 4 YOU**	PRINCE	WARNER BROTHERS	58	08	00
19.01.1985	**1999/ LITTLE RED CORVETTE**	PRINCE	WARNER BROTHERS	02	10	00
23.02.1985	**LET'S GO CRAZY/ TAKE ME WITH U**	PRINCE AND THE REVOLUTION	WARNER BROTHERS	07	10	00
25.05.1985	**PAISLEY PARK**	PRINCE AND THE REVOLUTION	WEA	18	12	00

DATE FIRST CHARTED	TITLE	ARTIST	LABEL	PEAK POSITION	WEEKS ON CHART	WEEKS @ NO.1
27.07.1985	RASPBERRY BERET	PRINCE AND THE REVOLUTION	WEA	25	09	00
26.10.1985	POP LIFE	PRINCE	PAISLEY PARK	60	02	00
08.03.1986	KISS	PRINCE	PAISLEY PARK	06	09	00
14.06.1986	MOUNTAINS	PRINCE AND THE REVOLUTION	PAISLEY PARK	45	06	00
16.08.1986	GIRLS AND BOYS	PRINCE AND THE REVOLUTION	PAISLEY PARK	11	09	00
01.11.1986	ANOTHERLOVERHOLE-NYOHEAD	PRINCE AND THE REVOLUTION	PAISLEY PARK	36	03	00
14.03.1987	SIGN 'O' THE TIMES	PRINCE	PAISLEY PARK	10	09	00
20.06.1987	IF I WAS YOUR GIRLFRIEND	PRINCE	PAISLEY PARK	20	06	00
15.08.1987	U GOT THE LOOK	PRINCE	PAISLEY PARK	11	09	00
28.11.1987	I COULD NEVER TAKE THE PLACE OF YOUR MAN	PRINCE	PAISLEY PARK	29	06	00
07.05.1988	ALPHABET STREET	PRINCE	PAISLEY PARK	09	06	00
23.07.1988	GLAM SLAM	PRINCE	PAISLEY PARK	29	04	00
05.11.1988	I WISH U HEAVEN	PRINCE	PAISLEY PARK	24	05	00
03.12.1988	KISS {1988}	PRINCE	NO-LABEL	76	01	00
27.05.1989	LITTLE RED COREVETTE/1999	PRINCE	NO-LABEL	92	01	00
24.06.1989	BATDANCE	PRINCE	WARNER BROTHERS	02	12	00
09.09.1989	PARTYMAN	PRINCE	WARNER BROTHERS	14	06	00
18.11.1989	THE ARMS OF ORION	PRINCE AND SHEENA EASTON	WARNER BROTHERS	27	07	00
04.08.1990	THIEVES IN THE TEMPLE	PRINCE	PAISLEY PARK	07	06	00
10.11.1990	NEW POWER GENERATION	PRINCE	PAISLEY PARK	26	04	00
31.08.1991	GETT OFF	PRINCE AND THE NEW POWER GENERATION	PAISLEY PARK	04	08	00
21.09.1991	CREAM	PRINCE AND THE NEW POWER GENERATION	PAISLEY PARK	15	07	00
07.12.1991	DIAMONDS AND PEARLS	PRINCE AND THE NEW POWER GENERATION	PAISLEY PARK	25	06	00
28.03.1992	MONEY DON'T MATTER 2 NIGHT	PRINCE AND THE NEW POWER GENERATION	PAISLEY PARK	19	05	00
27.06.1992	THUNDER	PRINCE AND THE NEW POWER GENERATION	PAISLEY PARK	28	03	00
18.07.1992	SEXY MF/STROLLIN'	PRINCE AND THE NEW POWER GENERATION	PAISLEY PARK	04	07	00
10.10.1992	MY NAME IS PRINCE	PRINCE	PAISLEY PARK	07	05	00
14.11.1992	MY NAME IS PRINCE (REMIXES)	PRINCE	PAISLEY PARK	51	01	00

DATE FIRST CHARTED	TITLE	ARTIST	LABEL	PEAK POSITION	WEEKS ON CHART	WEEKS @ NO.1
05.12.1992	**7**	**PRINCE AND THE NEW POWER GENERATION**	PAISLEY PARK	27	06	00
13.03.1993	**THE MORNING PAPERS**	**PRINCE AND THE NEW POWER GENERATION**	PAISLEY PARK	52	03	00
16.10.1993	**PEACH**	**PRINCE**	PAISLEY PARK	14	05	00
11.12.1993	**CONTROVERSY**	**PRINCE**	PAISLEY PARK	05	05	00
05.03.1994	**THE MOST BEAUTIFUL GIRL IN THE WORLD**	**PRINCE**	NPG	100	01	00
09.04.1994	**THE MOST BEAUTIFUL GIRL IN THE WORLD**	**(SYMBOL)**	NPG	01	13	02
04.06.1994	**THE BEAUTIFUL EXPERIENCE**	**(SYMBOL)**	NPG	18	05	00
10.09.1994	**LETITGO**	**PRINCE**	WARNER BROS	30	04	00
18.03.1995	**PURPLE MEDLEY**	**PRINCE**	WARNER BROS	33	02	00
23.09.1995	**EYE HATE U**	**(SYMBOL)**	WARNER BROS	20	03	00
09.01.1999	**1999**	**PRINCE**	WARNER BROS	10	09	00
20.11.2004	**CINNAMON GIRL**	**PRINCE**	COLUMBIA	43	02	00
08.04.2006	**BLACK SWEAT**	**PRINCE**	UNIVERSAL	43	02	00
10.06.2006	**FURY**	**PRINCE**	UNIVERSAL	60	01	00
07.07.2007	**GUITAR**	**PRINCE & THE NPG**	COLUMBIA	81	01	00
18.08.2007	**PURPLE RAIN**	**PRINCE & THE REVOLUTION**	WARNER BROS	62	07	00
15.02.2014	**PRETZELBODYLOGIC**	**PRINCE & 3RDEYEGIRL**	NPG	90	01	00

Discography taken from officialcharts.com

GOODNIGHT SWEET PRINCE

How the world reacted
to the loss of a legend...

"HE CHANGED THE WORLD! A TRUE VISIONARY. WHAT A LOSS. I'M DEVASTATED."

- MADONNA

"Today, the world lost a creative icon. Michelle and I join millions of fans from around the world in mourning the sudden death of Prince. Few artists have influenced the sound and trajectory of popular music more distinctly, or touched quite so many people with their talent. As one of the most gifted and prolific musicians of our time, Prince did it all. Funk. R&B. Rock and roll. He was a virtuoso instrumentalist, a brilliant bandleader, and an electrifying performer. 'A strong spirit transcends rules,' Prince once said, and nobody's spirit was stronger, bolder or more creative. Our thoughts and prayers are with his family, his band and all who loved him."

- BARACK OBAMA

"RIP OUR DEARLY BELOVED PRINCE. TEARS AND LOVE ON OUR TOUR BUS. I'LL NEVER FORGET MY BROTHER. WE'VE HAD GOOD TIMES."

- NILE RODGERS

"RIP PRINCE! ONE OF THE BEST OF ALL TIME! YOU WILL BE MISSED MY BROTHER."

- HUEY MORGAN

"Today is the worst day ever. I am crying."

- BOY GEORGE

"THIS IS TRULY DEVASTATING NEWS. THE GREATEST PERFORMER I HAVE EVER SEEN. A TRUE GENIUS. MUSICALLY WAY AHEAD OF ANY OF US. REST IN PEACE YOU PURPLE WARRIOR."

- SIR ELTON JOHN

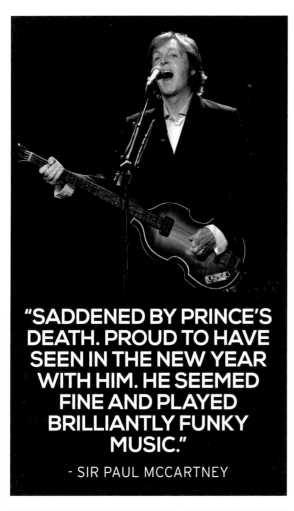

"PRINCE NOT ONLY CHANGED MY LIFE, BUT SAVED MY LIFE. MY HERO. HE IS THE FUNK."

- DAM FUNK

"THIS IS WHAT IT SOUNDS LIKE WHEN DOVES CRY. PRINCE RIP."

- WHOOPI GOLDBERG

"SADDENED BY PRINCE'S DEATH. PROUD TO HAVE SEEN IN THE NEW YEAR WITH HIM. HE SEEMED FINE AND PLAYED BRILLIANTLY FUNKY MUSIC."

- SIR PAUL MCCARTNEY

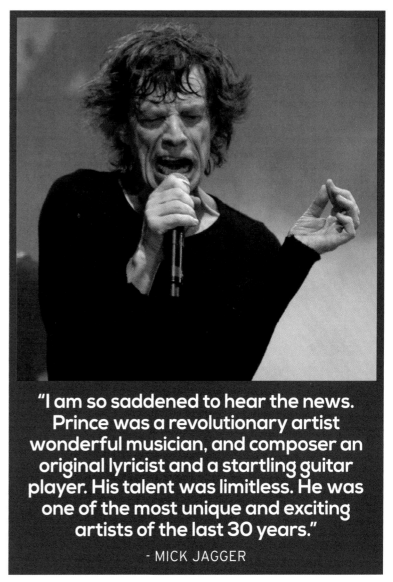

"I am so saddened to hear the news. Prince was a revolutionary artist wonderful musician, and composer an original lyricist and a startling guitar player. His talent was limitless. He was one of the most unique and exciting artists of the last 30 years."

- MICK JAGGER

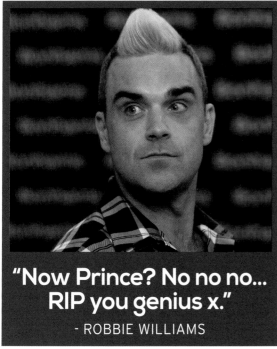

"Now Prince? No no no... RIP you genius x."

- ROBBIE WILLIAMS

"PRINCE. You legend. Rest In Peace."

- LILY ALLEN

"ALL THE DOVES TODAY. AND ME TOO. SO GRATEFUL FOR THE MUSICAL AND ARTISTIC REVOLUTION. FROM CHILDHOOD TO NOW. THANK YOU AND RIP PRINCE."

- CONNIE BRITTON

"PRINCE IS GONE, BUT THE MUSIC WILL GO ON ... AS I SAID, HE WAS JUST ONE OF THOSE ARTISTS THAT GO INTO THE STUDIO AND STAYED IN THE STUDIO. AND HE WOULD EVEN SLEEP IN THE STUDIO."

- ARETHA FRANKLIN

"THANK YOU GOD FOR LETTING US EXPERIENCE THE GREATNESS THAT IS PRINCE! WHAT A BLESSING!"

- KELLY ROWLAND

"Eric Clapton was asked about how it felt to be the world's best guitarist. His response: 'I don't know. Ask Prince'."

- STIG ABELL

"I'm Crushed!! UK news reporting Prince Is Dead?! For Real?! Massive Loss for us all! What a Genius! Speechless."

- SAMUEL L JACKSON

"I Miss My Brother. Prince Was A Funny Cat. Great Sense Of Humor."

- SPIKE LEE

"A MUSIC LEGEND PRINCE. THE WORLD HAS LOST A BIT OF MAGIC TODAY."

- EMMA BUNTON

'Rest in peace brother."
- IDRIS ELBA

"Musically, he could do it all: sing, play, arrange and produce."
- BRIAN WILSON

"We lost a visionary today. RIP Prince."
- MARK RUFFALO

"MY MUSICAL BROTHER... MY FRIEND...THE ONE WHO SHOWED ME THE POSSIBILITIES WITHIN MYSELF, CHANGED EVERYTHING, AND KEPT HIS INTEGRITY UNTIL THE END, IS GONE. I AM HEARTBROKEN."
- LENNY KRAVITZ

"It is impossible to imagine him not being here. The world of music was forever changed the day he picked up his guitar. His talent was breathtaking, his heart was kind, and all of us have been blessed to have had a glimpse into this sweet and magical soul."
- SHEENA EASTON